KING OF THE BAJA

© 2013 by Underground Voices
All rights reserved.

ISBN: 978-0-9830456-5-6

Printed in the United States of America.

INTRODUCTION
By Tony DuShane

Robert Guskind and I met online. We literary dated each other. The year was 2000 or as the cool kids called it, Y2K.

It was some awful website, I can't remember the name, but I remember my utter captivation of Guskind's stories. I also started the online literary 'zine Cherry Bleeds that year. It was a weekly 'zine and I asked Guskind if he would be a regular contributor. It was kind of like going to second base with him when he said yes.

We had four regular writers at the time and as the editor I wasn't accepting submissions yet. It was our way to bang out a story every week. I wanted new material from myself and the other writers. I called it Cherry Bleeds because I wanted to reference a Nick Cave song and I wanted to pop my cherry every time I wrote an article, story, and down the road, books, screenplays, etc.

Guskind and I were enthusiastic. Our online literary romance included discussing each other's work, asking each other for advice on how to punch our stories up. He was my literary brother three thousand miles away. We chatted about my topsy-turvy marriage and he told me of his romances and lost loves.

But our true love was for writing.

I knew Guskind was sober and I didn't ask him too much about that. He knew I was drinking away my problems and he didn't ask too much about that. In those early years he was worried who would read his work because he was chronicling and essentially confessing to earlier sins. I remember when we published the piece about him covering Jerry Brown for a publication and how he found a way to bounce up to Harlem to score dope and get his fix before heading back to meet Brown again a couple of hours later to finish the profile.

He was nervous about it and at the same time coming to terms with being okay with his identity. Who he was, who he became and the future that was looking pretty good.

Later, I started publishing Cherry Bleeds monthly because I was accepting submissions and couldn't keep up. Guskind wanted to keep up the weekly publication of his stories, so he kept turning out the material.

I believe there was a catharsis to diving into those stories and those times for him.

I'm not a fan of drug stories just for the sake of drug stories, just like I'm not a fan of erotica just for the sake of erotica. I'm a fan of honesty in writing. From the guts. And that's what Guskind had. Even if his life was on a different course and he was a vacuum salesman for years, I know his stories would have been just as compelling because in the end it's all about the human condition.

For a few years I begged him to submit his stories to agents and publishers. I had some connections and I wanted to give him an intro. He never took me up on my offer. There was something about rejection that he couldn't handle. I believe what he wrote was so personal that saying no to his stories would be saying no to his story, to his identity.

I said we could publish the book ourselves and I would put up the money. We released a Cherry Bleeds anthology called "Chemical Lust" instead. He was getting into photography. There was something more optimistic about him. He found love.

He told me his new girlfriend asked him to stop writing for Cherry Bleeds and to stop revisiting those stories. It was a point of conflict. If he made the decision himself I would have been fine with it, but he was trying to find a way around a woman and to keep publishing on Cherry Bleeds. The arrogant me told him to dump the woman.

I was the last man to talk as my marriage was about to unravel. Our literary love affair was bumpy for a while, but I always considered him my literary brother. When I threw all of my cards in and chucked my job and planned to write full time in Y2K, with utter delusion and earnest, he was my cheerleader and mentor. I wanted to write like him. I was happy he was a part of Cherry Bleeds and my life for so long.

My divorce was quite messy. It was the best and worst thing to happen to me. It was like losing my legs; then a year later I had bionic legs.

We reconnected a few days before he died, when I was going through my divorce and he was in the middle of his own issues. Our conversation was intense, and we were right back where we started. Even though life was giving us both a beating, it was like my brother had come home. We were in the playground again, ready to get messy, reconnected. Our creativity, our words would be our guides out of the sorrow of what makes us human.

His death hit me hard. When we chatted he said he felt like killing himself. I said he could come to San Francisco and stay with me or I could go to New York if he needed someone there. So, hearing the news that he was dead made me certain it was suicide. He was sober and it was a drug overdose. I guess we'll never know for certain.

After our chat I thought things were on the way to settling down for both of us. I felt like we could really do something together, something bigger than Cherry Bleeds ever was.

Over the years there were times I wanted to stop publishing Cherry Bleeds and he would talk me off the ledge. He was my self-help guru. When I felt like there was no meaning to what we were doing I would bump into someone at a party and they would tell me what a fan they were of Cherry Bleeds and especially of Robert Guskind and that they waited every Wednesday to read his next story.

Without Robert Guskind in our earthly existence I knew it was time to stop Cherry Bleeds. It was our bond. It was like a literary wedding ring. It hurts even now to know that one of the greats is gone.

What he wrote was great. What he had in him was even greater. He had so much more story to tell. He had an opus. He was so close to opening his heart and letting it spray literary gold to the world. If he had more time he would be mentioned right along with David Foster Wallace, William T. Vollmann and other contemporary writers receiving accolades as they deserve and as Robert Guskind deserved.

Don't just read his writing, devour it with every ounce of your soul because that's what Bob put into it.

-Tony DuShane, May 28, 2013

Tony DuShane is the author of *Confessions of a Teenage Jesus Jerk* (Soft Skull Press). He's a columnist for the San Francisco Chronicle and his essays and writing have appeared in Mother Jones and Penthouse. He also hosts the radio show Drinks With Tony.

KING OF THE BAJA
The writings of Robert Guskind

The night train from Stuttgart to Antwerp is rocketing through the German night at ninety miles an hour, leaving a trail of shit, piss and broken glass behind it.

I am standing in the WC, urinating and feeling no pain.

I finish whizzing and flush the toilet with a foot pedal. The metal bottom of the old school stainless steel Deutsche Bahn train toilet slips open; there's nothing beneath it but the rail bed rushing past in European darkness at high speed.

I listen to the Sisters of Mercy's Amphetamine Logic through my headphones:

Nothing but the knife to live for
One life all I need
Give me one good reason
Give me…
Amphetamine logic

I check my watch—it is nearly midnight. I zip up and reach into my pocket for another codeine and acetaminophen tablet—Tylenol with Balls—purchased after much persuasion of an unsympathetic pharmacist in Stuttgart and wash it down with the last hit of beer from my bottle of Lowenbrau. I press on the foot pedal again to open the toilet and toss the bottle down the hole.

The empty bottle rattles down the shit chute before slamming on to the tracks at 90 MPH.

This is a level of fun for a grown man, but it is the sort of thing that constitutes entertainment when you are drunk and buzzed on low-grade narcotics on a fuzzy all-night European train trip, tucked away in a second-class couchette compartment.

The trouble is that I am wide awake and there is no one with whom to play. My compartment mates—a guy who helps run a big zoo in the South and a top ranking official with one of the country's biggest urban parks departments—are fast asleep, having passed out cold after our umpteenth round of German beer, leaving me to wander the corridors of the Belgium-bound night train in a semi-drunken codeine haze, and to amuse myself by tossing empty bottles down the toilet onto the tracks.

I stumble back to the couchette car and crawl into my lower bunk. The Chicago park guy is snoring like a tractor-trailer. I lay on my back and stare at the ceiling, listening to his snores mix with the background noise of the speeding train.

When I open my eyes, the train is moving more slowly through the weak light of a very early morning spring sun.

Thank God.

We must be close to arriving in Antwerp. This is my first time in Antwerp, a Flemish port town that is a center of the international diamond trade. Other than knowing that Antwerp is where Reubens lived, that Reubensque as a descriptive term is derived from Reubens and that the beer kicks ass, it is fresh territory.

Antwerpen is the third stop on the walking tour of Europe in which I am participating, an all expense paid ten-day journey to see walking trails.

The English part of the trip is behind me, five days in the rain, exploring walking trails in the vicinity of Manchester, rediscovering the fact that I am not a walking through the woods or field kind of guy.

Walks in the forests of Merry Olde England and other countries are the price of being on this free trip. A group that wishes government to set aside more land for walking trails in the U.S.A., and to spend more building them, is paying for the trip. They hope I will go back to America and write nice things about trails, journalistic ethics be damned.

The trails in the U.K. were nice—the countryside was lush and green and the sheep and other livestock were very picturesque—but they're not my thing.

Arthur, the gray haired Brit leading the group of twelve has already told me he will have nightmares for years about a tall American man in a black trench coat following him through woods, howling about the mud and the bugs, demanding that the itinerary be changed to include downtown Manchester for 1980s British musical reasons, and listening to the Sisters of Mercy on his headphones.

Arthur lived through the Nazi Luftwaffe air raids and V2 missile attacks on Britain during World War II, but is beginning to look like he may not make it through a couple of weeks in the woods with me.

We have the rest of the day until a big group dinner scheduled for a place near Antwerp's small, but active, Red Light District. So a few hours after the train pulls into Antwerp, I set off from our hotel to explore Antwerp and try to re-up on drugs of some sort, as the Stuttgart supply of acetaminophen and codeine is rapidly being depleted.

I hit an atmospheric little café near Antwerp's towering cathedral, and quickly drink a couple of Westmalle Trappist Trippel beers, pre-lunch libations that will put the rest of the day in the proper perspective.

Sated, I wander down the Meir, an upper-end retail street, on a mission for narcotics.

My long black trench coat flaps in the wind as I scout for pharmacies.

There are many more walks through the woods to come in Belgium, Switzerland and France. Codeine is an excellent antidote for mud, vegetation and mosquitoes.

Still, the drug stores of Antwerp are a new territory for me. This is a potential problem—scoring prescription drugs from pharmacies in Europe can be amazingly simple, but it helps to know the turf.

I wander into a pharmacy—an apoteek—that looks like it hasn't changed since the early part of the Twentieth Century. It's all done up in dark wood and neat glass cases.

There are various containers full of powders and liquids behind the counter.

It is manned by a guy with gray hair who is wearing round wire-rimmed glasses and a white smock.

"Do you speak any English?" I say.

"Little bit," he says, pronouncing "bit" like "*beet.*"

"Maybe you can help me," I say. "I'm American…."

I pull out my passport and hold it up.

"And I'm here for a few days on a walking tour…"

"*Eh valkin' tur*?" the pharmacist says.

"I'm with a group," I say. "Walkers… uh… *wandelen*? *Grande Randonnée*? Rambling?"

I feel like a dork saying this, but it's central to my story.

"Ah, I *unterstant*," the pharmacist, who is staring at me intently, says. "*Dee voh-kink.*"

"And I have a problem with my knee," I say, patting my knee.

"A pro-*blam*?" he says.

"Pain," I say. "I have much pain. *Aiiiyyyy*! In the knee. And because I am walking so much it hurts. I'm probably going to have to have arthroscopic surgery on it at some point, but right now, I need a painkiller."

"*Peen kay-luhr*?" he says.

"Something to take away pain," I say. "Like codeine. That's what my American doctor recommends. You know codeine? Is there a Flemish word for it?"

Happy pill, perhaps? *De gelukkige pil*?

He looks at me blankly.

"Maybe you just call it codeine?" I continue. "I need some until I can see my doctor in the United States. Codeine to take pain away so that I can walk."

Jesus H. Christ.

Trying to get drugs is a demanding and time-consuming job.

A normal person would be going to museums looking at Flemish art.

Or shopping.

But not me.

I touch my knee and say, "*Aiiiyyy!*" again as though I'm a bizarre cartoon character trying to cop drugs in a foreign land with a strange combination of broken English, sound effects and pantomime. Like Marcel Marceau with sound looking for pharmaceuticals.

"You are *havink* pain?" he says.

"Severe pain in the knee," I say. "Terrible pain. Bad *aiiiyyy.*"

"Yes," he says. "I can *hilp peen.*"

"*Dank you,*" I say, trying to approximate "thank you" in Flemish. "*Dank you* so much. What a blessing. I've been in agony."

He looks in a drawer and hands me a small box.

"You *tek,*" he says. "*Hilps peen.*"

I pay him for the pills and pretend to limp slightly as I leave.

I'm practically in a cold sweat as I stand on the corner. I open the box, take out two of the small capsules and swallow them.

Then, I look at the box.

Mother of all fuckers.

It says something about homeopathic.

Homeopathic?

Like natural?

Holistic is fine, just not right now.

Screw homeopathic.

I want narcotic.

If I want homeopathic, I'll eat vegetation on one of my walks through the bloody woods.

I've swallowed a pill that probably contains dried lichen from Waterloo, powdered wildflowers from the Ardennes and ground Alpine Marmot claws.

Bite me.

I stop at a café, slump down at a table, order another Westmalle, drink it quickly and continue down the Meir.

I reenact my story a few minutes later at a more modern looking apoteek.

My reward is two red-and-yellow metal tubes of codeine and acetaminophen tablets.

Now we're talking.

A few minutes later, I walk out of another apoteek two blocks away with an additional tube.

Ten minutes after that comes another tube from another apoteek.

Etc.

An hour-and-a-half later, there are so many metal tubes of codeine tablets in my coat that the pockets look like they have rocks in them and I clink as I walk.

I stop at a café, sit down at a table and order another strong Belgian beer. I take a codeine tablet and wash it down with the triple-strength brew made by Belgian monks.

By the time I make it back to the hotel, I am very much the jolly walking dude.

Arthur is in the lobby. He looks at me and asks me in his English accent where I've been.

"Walking all over Antwerp," I say.

"Quite the city walker, aren't you?" he says.

"I love walking in the city, Arthur," I say. "It's the woods that suck."

*

The codeine tablets I copped from the pharmacy on the Keyserlei in Antwerp are definitely the thing.

They are, in fact, the perfect accompaniment to the Westmalle Trappist Trippel beer I am drinking in a café on a cobblestone back street near the atmospheric and towering gothic Cathedral of Our Lady. Indeed, the Xanax is putting the beer and codeine buzz in a properly mellow perspective.

Before repairing to the warmth and comfort of my café, I smoked about half of a thick hash and tobacco cigarette while wandering the streets of old Antwerp.

All of these substances are proving to be exactly what the doctor ordered, in exactly the right combination.

In the perfect place.

At an ideal time.

Specifically, Thanksgiving Day.

It is not Thanksgiving in Belgium, just another Thursday—and a damned cold one at that.

This is fine with me.

Here in Antwerp, an icy and unforgiving Northern European pre-winter wind is whipping off the River Scheldt. The streets and squares are packed with people. And the traffic is on the nasty side.

Christmas lights and decorations are going up.

Artists are painting intricate Santa Clauses—*Sinterklaas* in Flemish—in shop windows.

There are the beginnings of Christmas markets in several squares.

The holidays in Europe are more dignified and, well, European than what you get back in the States—Christmas decorations that go up before Halloween making for an unsettling sense of Permanent Yuletide, guys in Santa suits sitting under garishly decorated plastic trees in the center courts of shopping malls surrounded by mechanical reindeer and short, thin chicks playing the role of elves. Etc.

Yes, the European holiday scene is far better.

I'm smoking a pungent Gitane and woozily contemplating my surroundings, which—thanks to the Trappist monks who brew the beer, the pharmaceutical company biochemists who concoct the codeine and Xanax and the South Asians who make the kick-ass Black Hash sold all over Amsterdam—are very interesting indeed.

The place in which I am parked is called *Het Elfde Gebod.*

Het Elfde Gebod is Flemish for "The 11th Commandment."

The meaning of this oblique reference is beyond me. Although I was obligated to study theology as part of a Jesuit education at Georgetown, I am not terribly Biblical—and certainly not in a scholarly sense—except for the way I consume liquor and drugs, which has a very Old Testament aura about it.

Het Elfde Gebod has bare brick walls and heavy wood beams, and it is full of religious artifacts.

Angels suspended from the ceiling.

Statues of saints and the Madonna.

Stained glass windows.

And a long, long list of ambrosia-like Belgian brews, some of them with names like Lucifer and Judas, from which to choose. With classical music as the backdrop.

Belgian beer is God's way of telling man that only a handful of peoples have any business brewing beer and that Americans are not among them.

Spending quality time with beer and drugs in *Het Elfde Gebod* is my idea of the perfect Thanksgiving. No travel hassles. No monstrous and pesky family issues. No tugs of war with significant others to determine with whose family and in which region you will pass the holiday this year.

It's a pity the Old World became so miserable that refugees inflicted themselves, and a holiday they created celebrating the subjugation of indigenous peoples, on the

New World. The important thing is that, for some reason, God spared Europe the gluttonous excess, familial agony and traveling horror of Thanksgiving. Not to mention the extraordinarily unique modern American torment of having to watch the Detroit Lions play on Thanksgiving year after year after year after year.

I am resolutely staying on the other side of the Atlantic until this all passes, and having a damned good time doing it.

I am staying at an anonymous and cheap hotel in Brussels that is often frequented by rock bands touring on a budget, and hanging out with my friend Laurence, who is Swiss-born, tall and blonde. She works for a cool record label based in Brussels. On Saturday, Laurence and I are hitting a wedding reception for the bass player of a Belgian speed metal band that is taking place at a rock club in Brussels.

I have a super high alcohol beer called a Last Judgment, get the check from my waiter and head back out to the frigid streets of Antwerp. There are several pharmacies I want to visit in order to stock up on extra codeine and acetaminophen AKA Percocet in the United States. One can never have too many narcotic painkillers.

In Antwerp, Brussels and other Belgian cities, all you have to do is walk into a pharmacy and claim a toothache, backache or some other vague and troubling malaise involving the kind of ache codeine can dull and you walk out with a healthy supply of codeine tablets.

Codeine is an over-the-counter medication in many European countries. This is yet another reason that Europe, and specifically Belgium, is such a wonderful and magical place.

After I score more drugs, I'll catch a five or six o'clock train back to Brussels and hook up for dinner with Laurence somewhere in the vicinity of the magnificent Grand-Place.

An *apotheken*—a drug store—is up ahead on the right.

I have done this, quite literally, a hundred times in a dozen countries in Europe, leading me to know as much about specific pharmacies in certain cities as some people know about art galleries and restaurants. I know which ones are almost no questions asked, which hassle you slightly while ultimately giving you what you ask for, which ones tell you to come back with a local doctor's prescription and which, basically, tell you to take a hike—no script equals no pills and, no, we don't know a doctor you can visit to get one.

I assume a studied expression of prolonged suffering due to a penetrating ache begging for narcotic amelioration and move in for the score.

A middle-aged woman with blonde hair from a bottle looks up at me from beneath thick glasses.

"Hello," I smile. "Do you speak English?"

"*A lee-tell*," she says.

"Good. Maybe you can help me. I'm American and I'm in Belgium for the next month…"

She looks at me curiously and says, "Yes?"

"I have a terrible back problem. It's been going on for months. I think it's a herniated disc, but I'm not sure."

"Yes?"

The pharmacist is tugging at her white smock.

"I take a drug in the United States called Percocet for the pain. Have you heard of it?"

"*Pear-koh-sets*?"

"Yes! It's codeine and acetaminophen or codeine and aspirin, in which case it's called Percodan."

"*Ah so*. Codeine. I know this medication."

"Well, I hate to take it. You know, it just isn't good to take too much. But, I forgot all my pills in the U.S. and my prescription is there too. I'm in pain and I need some pills for the month I'll be here. Do you know a doctor?"

"For the pain?" she says.

"Well, I have a doctor for that in the United States. Really, I need a prescription for the codeine."

"Ah, this is no problem. You do not need this in Belgium. I can give you these…"

She reaches into a drawer and pulls out a little metal cylindrical container that looks like something that could hold very large breath mints administered by the dose, except that the package design, which is yellow and white lettering on a red background, is clearly more utilitarian and pharmaceutical in nature than something that kills doggy breath.

"There are *twelff* in here," she says. "I can *giff* you more if you wish."

"Yeah," I say. "Like I said, I hate taking this stuff. I don't think it's very good for you in the long run, but I'm going to be here a month."

She reaches into the drawer, pulls out two more cylinders of codeine pills and says, "I *giff* you *twelff* more or *twelff* more than this."

"Hmm," I say, doing my best not to smile or drool. "Maybe the twelve and the twelve more. That should be enough."

"Very well."

She puts the three containers in a small bag, hands them to me and asks for the equivalent of fifteen dollars. I hand over the cash and thank her for her help.

"It is nothing," she says. "If you are here and you are in need of more, you return. I *giff* you more."

I thank her profusely, turn and leave.

I nearly dance down the sidewalk, where workmen are stringing tasteful little white lights on shrubs.

This may not be a traditional Thanksgiving, but I, for one, am thankful.

Sinterklaas is coming to town

Sinterklaas is coming to town. He is, in fact, visible all over Amsterdam.

The Dutch Santa Claus, *Sinterklaas*, a centuries old character upon whom our own Santa is based, arrived in town by boat a few weeks ago. He had a huge parade through town accompanied by a horde of elves in blackface, live on Dutch National TV.

Now, his visage, more religious icon-like in appearance and a good deal more svelte than our own St. Nick adorns many windows.

I see evidence of this in the days leading up to Christmas whenever I'm motivated to forsake my tan Afghani heroin-induced internal reveries and venture forth from my warm and cozy hotel room overlooking the Herengracht, the Gentleman's Canal.

I tend to come out at night, which is an easy thing to do, since the chilly Northern European sun comes up late and starts going down around four in the afternoon in Amsterdam in late December, when there are barely eight hours of daylight.

Currently, it's a little before ten and I'm firmly rooted to a seat in the Tea Room on the top floor of the Melkweg, an Amsterdam club and performance space.

Parakeets and other caged birds are chirping away, their tweet-tweets clearly audible above some chill electronica sounds and the din of conversation.

The Tea Room is getting crowded. An assortment of people of different ages, sizes, shapes and nationalities are sitting on benches and chairs around the room in various stages of inebriation, both chemical and alcohol. A thick cloud of cannabis, hashish and tobacco smoke hovers overhead.

I'm nursing a Duvel, a high-octane Belgian beer in a fat, brown glass bottle, and looking around the Tea Room from behind bloodshot eyes with heroin pupils the size of pinpricks.

My high tolerance for drugs and alcohol is serving me well tonight. I've smoked most of a fat hash-and-tobacco cigarette. I've consumed two Duvels. And, I've done another thick line of good, strong Afghani dope within the last two hours. Before, I headed out to dinner at a venerable Indonesian restaurant on Leidsestraat near the frigid and windblown Leidseplein, where I pigged out on a massive rijstafel dinner.

An Indonesian rijstafel feast tastes very good when you're in the middle of a heroin binge.

I've been doing about half a gram of strong Afghani smack for about a week, and I've finally settled into a comfortable groove that allows me to resume normal life functions like eating and sleeping, after many days of being unable to do either. Of course, this is a strong indication that I'm now strung out and will become monstrously ill if and when I stop doing dope, but that is a problem I will face in the indeterminate future, most likely after I return to the U.S. after New Year's.

The United States is always where the shit hits the fan.

Right now, as I lounge in the Tea Room, dope sickness is an ill-formed dark cloud barely visible over the horizon.

A couple of young blondes—one with shoulder-length hair and the other with short-cropped hair in a pixie cut, and both of them with sinuous physiques—are sitting across from me, languorously smoking a hashish and tobacco cigarette. They are Danish or Swedish from the sound of their conversation. A mixed group of Amsterdammers and tourists is carrying on an animated discussion over on the next group of high-back padded benches arranged around low, round tables.

It is time for a Space Cake, the Amsterdam version of hash brownies. They taste awful, like a hideously concocted and baked brownie mixed with dirt, but that's okay. Space Cakes are not about taste. They are about the inner glow that follows.

I walk over to the bar where the bartenders dish out Space Cakes along with beer, coffee, tea and other liquors, and ask for two Space Cakes, which I consume quickly and wash down with Duvel.

I ask one of the blondes to my right where she's from, and it turns out they're Danes from Copenhagen.

The blonde with long hair is named Greta and the one with the pixie cut is Eva. They've been in Amsterdam for several days checking out the party scene. Both are urban planning students in Copenhagen.

Urban planning?

The Melkweg is the kind of place where you run into spaced-out backpackers in Amsterdam for drugs, sex and rock-and-roll holidays, not aspiring urban planners.

"Planning, *really*?" I say.

"Yes," Eva says. "It is good *subject*, but very boring."

Her Scandinavian accent leads her to pronounce her j's as y's—as in "*subyecht*"—and her o's like ah—as in "*bahring*" instead of "boring."

"Not at all," I say. "I know a little bit about planning. I've written for Planning. It's a magazine."

"I have read this *yuhrnal*," Greta says.

"You really read Planning?"

"*Ja*, this is true."

Who would have thought?

"You are here for Christmas?" Greta asks.

"Yeah," I say. "This is my first Christmas with *Sinterklaas*."

"Ah. In Denmark, we have *Jule Mander*."

"*Jule Mander*?"

"Ja. He is like your Santa Claus. Is same *pahrson* with different name."

"Fat and happy?"

"*Ja.* Not like *Sinterklaas.*"

"Yeah. I don't know about Sinterklaas. Creepy elves."

And, potentially, racist in some circles.

"We call this elfs in Denmark, *Jul Nisse,*" she says. "They live in the attic."

Ah, well. To each culture its own creepy nuances.

Greta and Eva announce they want Space Cakes, so we get and eat another round of them. Then, I roll a hashish and tobacco joint the size of a cigar and we pass it around until we we're all coughing and red-faced.

Greta wonders if there are any good raves around, which I'm absolutely not up for. I suggest we go downstairs to dance.

We go down to the first floor. The club is even more crowded than it was earlier. A loud and fairly obnoxious punk band is playing onstage. The crowd is divided into two groups. There's a thrashing, moshing mob in front of the stage. Behind that is a group that is alternately thrashing and dancing or standing and watching. They are surging back and forth like seaweed propelled by underwater currents, depending on the movement of the mob in front of them.

This is where we go.

Eva hangs on to me for a bit, but the crowd tosses us around.

We are pushed forward.

We are thrust backward.

We are slammed sideways.

We go in very different directions and all end up dancing with ourselves.

Eventually, I retreat to the back bar. I am drenched in sweat. My feet ache from having been stomped on several times. There is a bump on my left arm where I hit God only knows what in my ricochets around the dance floor.

I get a Heineken and watch the maelstrom in front of me, feeling unspeakably stoned and staggeringly drunk.

The Danish females to whom I have no attachment and to whom I will likely have none as they leave for Copenhagen in the morning, are still thrashing away. I catch Greta's eye and wave goodbye. She waves and blows me a kiss.

I emerge from the Melkweg on to the frigid streets of Amsterdam and walk in the general direction of my hotel, but get confused, and end up on the fringes of Amsterdam's Red Light District. It is in full swing.

Now that I'm here, I will have a look see.

I walk up the Oude Zijds Achterburgwal, one of the two main canals that run through the neighborhood. It is ablaze with a rainbow of brightly lit signs advertising sex shops, porn shops, peep shows, live sex shows, nude bars, smoking cafés, souvenir shops and head shops. And, of course, dozens and dozens of scantily clad women of all ethnic persuasions are sitting in shop windows under red and pink lights.

I stroll the length of the other main canal, the Oude Zijds Voorburgwal, and wander into the myriad of narrow, cobblestone back streets and alleys that make up the heart of the Red Light District.

The mostly male crowd is rough and drunk, and clearly on the prowl.

I duck into a doorway on a quiet back alley, surreptitiously snort another line of heroin off the back of my hand and head back to the O.Z. Voorburgwal. The porn shops cater to every imaginable kink and fetish. And, now, many of them are decorated with twinkling Christmas lights. There are store windows filled with sex toys that attest to the boundless nature of human erotic tastes—leather, chains, latex, masks, studded collars, cock rings, discipline balls, nipple clamps, whips, vibrators, immense phalluses, grotesque blow-up dolls and toys catering to the straight, gay, bi, dominant, submissive, top, bottom, sadistic, masochistic, etc., etc., etc.

The dope and hash and alcohol are now clearly kicking my ass. One of the sex shops has an elaborate Christmas display in the window, including a *Sinterklaas* doll unlike any other I've seen in Amsterdam or anywhere else.

Sinterklaas is on all fours. His dark red pants are around his ankles. A doll dressed as an elf in black face is behind him.

The elf is violating *Sinterklaas's* bum with a large, bright red phallus.

Ho ho ho, indeed.

I shake my head and chuckle. It's definitely time to retire.

I turn in the direction of the Herengracht and walk through the icy wind back toward my hotel.

Le Deluge

The Italian Dolomite Alps have the unmistakable look of the slow fade to fall.

Whenever I drift out of my deep opiate nod and into hazy consciousness, I look out the window of the train compartment—a first-class smoker that I, thankfully, have to myself—and see dark pewter clouds obscuring the tops of the craggy mountains and foliage that is turning to earth tones. The clouds are lower and darker every time I reluctantly open my eyes.

A storm is moving into this part of Europe from the Adriatic.

A half-hour into the mountains, a steady rain erupts from the sodden clouds. It turns the Alpine gloom darkly beautiful in a way that matches the vibe I'm feeling from my heroin buzz.

I'm very wasted on tan Afghani dope, but more in a depressed way than a giddy one. When I'm doing dope, everything in the world and in life revolves around it. If I have a large supply on hand, I am carefree. If the end is in sight, I am sullen.

Après héroine, le deluge.

I procured a large quantity of dope in Zurich, enough to easily see me through Berlin and beyond. It would have been enough to cover me for my entire trip, except that my rate of consumption has been increasing exponentially every day.

I spent the first part of the train ride—before lapsing into a state that makes reasoning impossible—trying to devise ways to ration the remaining drugs. To the point of jotting down bizarre little equations on a yellow legal pad in a futile attempt to pre-plan my consumption and conserve dope. If I can stick to my desperate conservation plan, I will make it back to Zurich in just enough time to score more drugs.

The odds of the plan working, however, are significantly less than fifty-fifty. *Having* less dope does not necessarily lead me to *do* less dope, just to *wish* that I'd do less of it. Despite the dwindling supply, I'm still putting so much tan powder up my nose that I can't remember what I'm doing most of the time, except that I know that I'm spending an inordinate amount of time worrying that I'm going to run out of dope.

I've been on a train since I boarded this morning in Berlin. The final destination, around midnight, is Venice.

Venice is an atmospheric and wonderful place, and I make a point of going there as often as I can. Now, I'm dreading it because Venice is a shitty town for dope.

A Venetian friend told me that there were a handful of local heroin addicts in Venice and that they hung out in an obscure and out-of-way piazza, but that the cops rousted them and they're not there anymore.

The nearest dope spots that I know of are in *Milan.*

I won't be in Milan until I pass through on my way to Zurich. By then, it will be a done deal.

I will either scrape through by the skin of my teeth or I'll arrive in Zurich—via another scenic train trip through the Swiss Alps—dope sick, shivering and puking.

I've been snorting up strong dope like a vacuum cleaner for nearly two weeks, so I'm now mightily strung out, despite my firm intention to avoid this fate and to stop using heroin entirely. After my last hideous withdrawal episode several months ago, I threw out about a quarter of a gram of stupendously powerful red Pakistani heroin, swearing that I'd never, ever, ever touch anything again in my life with the power to make me that sick and miserable.

Then, I reconsidered and arrived at a compromise—I swore off using dope for more than three days in a row so that I could do dope, but not get strung out. Three days being, according to junkie folk wisdom, the maximum period of time you can do heroin without developing a jones and experiencing withdrawal symptoms—real or imagined—when you stop. Now, I wonder how I could have been so insane as to throw away some of the strongest dope upon which I have ever laid my hands.

So much for plans.

My long-term goal, at this point, is to avoid withdrawal until I'm back in the United States, since getting dope sick in Europe would have a definite adverse impact on my travels.

Some people come home from trips abroad with odd gastrointestinal maladies.

Or *tchotchkes.*

Or snapshots.

Or very long distance girlfriends.

I bring home an abominable dope habit.

Outside, the downpour becomes more intense near the Brenner Pass. If this keeps up, Venice—which is built on sinking islands in the middle of a lagoon off the Adriatic—will be intensely gloomy and sodden.

I sigh and consider the bright side.

I have friends in Venice. A redheaded former investment banker chick from Cincinnati who makes cool jewelry. A Venetian guy who runs a little hole-in-the-wall restaurant where we have all-night drinking and bullshitting sessions.

Venice will be fun.

As long as the dope holds out.

We pass through Bolzano.

It's raining harder.

We hit Trento.

There's practically a monsoon coming down.

The downpour becomes even more torrential as we get to Verona, and I start to wonder if the Italian news is featuring footage of formerly picturesque villages sliding down mountainsides.

I hit the fetid toilet and do another couple of lines of dope while the train is sitting in the station at Verona and, then, head back to my seat. There's a little more than an hour left before we hit the *Stazione Santa Lucia* in Venice.

I slump back into my seat and light up a Marlboro. The train pulls out of the station. I put out the cigarette and close my eyes.

The next thing I know, the train is stopped and quiet. It is sitting at the platform in Santa Lucia.

Damn. I must have nodded off. I wonder how long we've been in the station?

The train lurches like an engine is being connected or cars are being removed.

I spring to life and grab my bags. One of them is weighted down with five bottles of boutique brands of schnapps I copped in Munich.

I sprint through the train in one of those just-woke-up hazes compounded by a really solid dope buzz, desperate to get off before it starts moving and I have to escape from an Italian rail yard.

I get to the door and take a step down the stairs.

This is when gravity conspires with my own questionable equilibrium and takes over.

Damn.

The heavy bag pulls me off the stairs and down to the platform.

The swan dive to the concrete below happens in that nasty, disembodied sort of slow motion that occurs whenever something truly bad takes place. It's not unlike going to the instant replay and watching it happen to someone else. Particularly in my frame of mind.

Fuck.

It occurs to me to drop the bag—the hell with breaking the bottles of designer German booze—but this does nothing to lessen my becoming one with the platform.

Double fuck.

I hit the platform on my left side, roll once and end up on my back staring at the dirty awning overhead.

Now I know where the pigeons live at Santa Lucia.

I've staggered off a train or two in my time, but I've never *fallen* off one before.

I move my legs.

I check my arms.

I feel for any warm fluids that would be blood.

It doesn't feel like anything is broken and I don't seem to be bleeding.

"Are you okay?" a guy shouts in Italian.

"*Unnnhhh*," I say.

"Are you okay?" he says again.

"*Uhhhhhh*."

"Are you hurt?"

"No."

"That was a bad fall," he says.

"Yeah."

"Big fall."

"Si," I say. My left side feels like I just fell three feet and became one with the platform. "*Bottiglie di schnapps. Tedeschi*."

Bottles of schnapps. German.

"Schnapps?" he says.

I explain that I have five large bottles of schnapps (peach, apple, pear, etc.) in my shoulder bag and that I tripped, the extra weight causing me to interact poorly with gravity.

He nods, looks down at me, offers his hand and helps me to my feet.

"*Grazie*," I say.

"*Prego*," he says.

I pick up my bags and drag my bruised body down the platform, through the deserted station and out to the stop for the *vaparetto*—Venetian waterbuses that are boats that function like buses—on the Grand Canal.

Venice is warm and damp, although the deluge has stopped.

My destination is the Hotel Marconi, which is on the Riva del Vin on the Grand Canal near the Rialto Bridge. My jewelry designer friend Ami got the room for me at a very reduced rate because she and the owner are friends.

Normally, I'm excited when I arrive in Venice, feeling like I've exited the real world and entered a very special one. I relish the boat ride down the Grand Canal.

Not tonight. I simply want to get to the hotel and die. A vaparetto arrives. I board and look glumly at the darkened *palazzi* lining the canal.

The deluge has started again by the time the vaparetto gets to the stop at the Rialto Bridge. It's almost one in the morning.

Venice is magnificently deserted.

I open an umbrella and trudge through the pouring rain and murk along the Grand Canal, sorely tempted to throw the German booze that almost killed me into the water. I drag myself through the entrance to the Hotel Marconi and into the little lobby full of antiques.

A sleepy looking guy in a nice, dark Italian suit looks up. He stares at me curiously.

I catch a glimpse of myself in a mirror. I look like I've been through a war.

"Long train ride," I say in Italian. "I came from Berlin."

"Very long," he says.

I give him my name. He finds my reservation. We do the paperwork.

He hands me the key to my room. It's a nice room, he says. It is on the third floor.

No bellhop. No elevator.

I thank him and start the long trudge up the Venetian staircase, calculating how much dope I should do before bedtime and wondering how long the rainstorm outside will last and how many days I will be in Venice before I run out of dope and the deluge inside begins.

Zurich

It is cold, gloomy and wet in Zurich. It has been raining so hard, for so many days, in fact, that Zurich is starting to remind me of Dublin or Manchester or Seattle.

The weather, however, is bright and sunshiny compared to my mood, which is so dark and foul that if I were a place, I would be *Die Unterwelt.*

The Underworld.

In point of fact, I am so down that I wish I were *Toten in die Unterwelt*, or however one says, "I wish I were dead in Hell" in Swiss German as opposed to German German.

It is, no doubt, different.

Everything is.

Even the fine South Asian dope—the "Sugar"—I have purchased in Zurich that is coursing through my veins hasn't wiped away the funk, even if it has made the vicissitudes of life somewhat easier to bear.

The Sugar I've been sniffing in large quantity—and I've got two grams of the sandy colored powder with which to work—is very banging shit, as they say, although the vernacular in Zurich is different.

The fact is, I should be feeling no pain. My main emotion as I stare at the storm clouds that are obscuring the Alps far beyond the Zurichsee, should be something along the lines of:

Wheeeeee.

Or,

Whaaalllaaaa.

Or,

Lalalalalalalalalalalalala.

Or,

Deedadeedadeedadeedadeedadeedadeeda.

But, it is not.

I stop on a sodden street corner and observe the panorama of the Bellevueplatz, and the blue Zurich streetcars rumbling in and out in the torrential rain.

I take a Xanax from my pocket, put it in my mouth and swallow it with saliva. A couple of hours ago I purchased 100 Xanax without prescription, just a long bogus speech about oppressive anxiety and nervousness, from a pharmacy on Bahnhofstrasse, the street lined by Swiss banks and hyper-expensive stores that is Zurich's miracle mile.

The Xanaxes—generic name alprazolam from the benzodiazepine family, the biochemical anti-anxiety agents that are God's apology to mankind for making the world a shitty and tense place—are just .5 milligram ones.

I walked into a drugstore and got 100 of them without a script. For way less money than they cost in the USA.

I have already eaten two of them. The one I just popped is my third.

I am a touch resistant to Xanax, having built up significant tolerance to them. Whereas, a milligram of Xanax is enough to send the average person to Happy Land or knock him or her on his or her ass, I can swallow a couple of milligrams and still be wide awake. Wired, in fact, if I chase them with espresso.

I do not know why God has granted me such admirable tolerance to most substances. I would have given anything to be one of those people that get wasted on nothing.

Yet, despite the heroin and the alprazolam—which should foster a ha-ha, happy, devil may care, who gives a fuck attitude—I am in the depths of deep and despondent depression.

Fuck it all straight to die *unterwelt.*

The cause of this angst is a female named Gabi from Munich.

Blonde, young and pretty in that young, blonde German *fraulein* way, Gabriella from Munich was supposed to get on a train and meet me in Zurich.

She is not here, nor will she be.

Why, in fact, should she be?

The sum total of my experience with Gabi amounts to six or so hours over the course of two hours in a shady bar near Munich's hauptbahnhof making out with her. Before I left Munich, she proposed coming to join me in Zurich and, then, possibly accompanying me back to the Good Old USA.

Never mind that importing this blonde Bavarian chick to America might not be the best of moves—and that it would certainly be a decision made in haste.

It would have been what it would have been and, in point of fact, it would have been a bad idea.

Heroin, however, as any junkie prone to occasional reflection knows, interferes with the body in many, many ways; it shuts down some of its most important functions, starting with the ability to digest food and defecate and moving on to all of its psycho-emotional aspects.

Heroin = Clouded Judgment.

Heroin + Liquor = Mush Brain.

Heroin + Liquor + Xanax = Huh?

What?

Was I saying something?

S'up?

Why are you looking at me like that, dude?

Hence, making plans with Gabriella from Munich.

Alas, when I called the number she gave me, a German man answered.

"Is Gabi there?" I said.

He said something German that I didn't understand.

"Gabriella, she is there, *bitte*?" I said, slowly, approximating the diction of someone who doesn't speak

English for the benefit of someone who doesn't understand English.

He screamed things in German that were undoubtedly foul and vulgar; I could tell by the tone of his voice.

Yes, Gabi is a memory—one that will no doubt disappear from RAM thanks to heroin, liquor, Xanax or another substance that causes loss of data or, God Forbid, a control-alt-delete reboot situation—unless I want to double back to Munich.

I'm in a bad way.

I miss Gabi's mangled German-infused diction.

Excited I am bekomink from you.

In America, you ist doing vhat?

To Zurich I am komink.

Etc.

I want to speak broken English with Gabi, so I can say things like:

A long time for you I am waiting.

And

In Zurich, with me in my hotel you will stay.

Unrequited love sucks.

So too, unrequited lust.

I hop on a tram and head to my buddy Richard's soul food restaurant and blues club on Zypressenstrasse, which is in a part of Zurich with a large population of Turks, Serbs and other immigrant workers.

The restaurant doesn't open for hours yet, but I bang on the door and Magbul, Richard's Afghani bartender—with whom I have bonded over late night drinks at a dance club near the Zurich airport—lets me in. Magbul invites me to wait upstairs in the boss's office.

He should be there any minute.

I sit at Richard's desk. The next thing I know, someone is saying, "Wake up."

"Huh?" I say.

"You're out like a light," Richard says. "Wake up."

No kidding. What does he expect?

A great deal of the dope has traveled up my nose.

I have no reason or desire to be lucid; it defeats the purpose of doing heroin.

I open my eyes. I can smell the ribs that a couple of the Pakistani chefs are cooking in the tiny kitchen down the hall.

Outside, a steady drizzle is still falling.

My first thought is, why is Richard fucking with my nod and bringing me back to the depressing Swiss land of rain? I was happy and content in the Land of Nod.

"You know," Richard says. "I've told you a million times that you can't do dope here and nod out like that."

"I was asleep," I say. "What's the big deal? Everybody nods on dope."

"Because everybody's going to know you're high."

"C'mon. Nobody cares."

"I do."

Like Richard doesn't do dope and consume vast quantities of alcohol.

"Give me a break," I whine. "I'm depressed."

"Are you still bummed about the German chick?"

"Yup."

Richard gets up and puts a Robert Cray album into the CD player in his office.

"Forget about her," he says. "She took you for a ride."

"I really dug her," I say.

"Give me a break. You were the shill."

"The shill?"

"The shill. The mark. The victim. It was a scam, bro. She's a bargirl. She works in the place. The whole point is to get you to spend a lot of money buying her drinks. You know how many guys have gotten drunk and engaged to bargirls? It happens all the time."

"I don't get it, though. I was leaving the next day. So, why bother with the phone number and all that? You really think it was a scam?"

I'm not sure what's worse. Knowing I was conned. Being dumb enough to believe the chick was going to show up in Zurich. Or telling Richard I got suckered.

"It's a classic set up," he says. "Cheer up. It happens to everybody."

"Did it ever happen to you?"

"Not that way, but I've blown plenty of money when I'm drinking. It's nothing. Can you afford what you spent on her?"

"Yeah."

"Well, then chalk it up to experience," he says. "Hang out tonight. There are plenty of girls around. Swiss girls from rich families. Rich girls are fun too. You should give them a chance."

"Is Jill around?"

Jill is an American from Laguna Beach who lives in Zurich and teaches grade school. I have had an interest in her.

"Yeah," Richard says. "She's still drinking too much and she's back with Firooz."

Firooz is Jill's on-again, off-again photographer boyfriend who comes with a reputation for a lot of slimy dealings with the models he shoots.

"Cool," I say.

"She *lives* at the bar," he says. "My advice to you, Skippy, is forget about her."

I tell Richard that I've got to split.

I'm hooking up for a couple of drinks with a German jewelry designer I know through my ex-girlfriend; he lives right over the border near Schaffhausen.

Unfortunately, this means that now that I've worked hard on getting wasted, I will have to try to look as straight as possible.

This is not good planning on my part, but it is part of the Curse of the Junkie.

Fritjof, the jewelry designer, shows up at my hotel at the appointed hour with his wife, Sabina.

We drive off, as I consider my options.

I can go back to the States to recharge my batteries, and return to Zurich when I am happier.

I can continue to hang in Zurich, and pursue Jill or another as yet unknown female.

I can hang out with Richard.

Or,

I can hang out with myself and spend days on end in a drug and alcohol induced haze.

Decisions. Decisions.

In the meantime, there's tonight with my German friends.

KING OF THE BAJA

The view from the two-story, floor-to-ceiling glass wall in our house atop a cliff abutting the Pacific Ocean in the Baja California is a magnificent panorama of the green-gray sea and Coronado Island.

I have repaired to the Baja, where my buddy from Zurich, Richard, is living in his family's oceanfront home to write a novel and beat back a nasty dope habit.

Nothing doing.

So far, I've only co-written a short story with Richard. Meanwhile, the monkey I had on my back when I arrived from Washington is finding the rarified air south of the border to his liking. In less than a month, he's grown from a chimp into a large, red-assed baboon that regularly demands significant quantities of the brown Mexican tar they sell up in the hills east of Rosarito—a honky-tonk beach town a half-hour south of Tijuana—in ten dollar pellets that look like rat turds.

I get off the phone with my editor in Washington having bought a delay of another week on the story I'm supposed to send him to justify the paycheck he sends me that enables my *vida* Mexicana. I could care less about work and writing right now. My body has taken to demanding heroin on a regular schedule and I need my afternoon infusion of dope. Badly.

Without dope and the normalcy it brings, I will be less than human by nightfall.

I ask Richard if he wants to go on a drug run with me.

He shrugs and says that he's going to stay home to do laundry.

Would I mind picking up a few *curas*—which is what they call the pellets of brown dope—for him?

"No problem," I say.

"Why don't you drive up to see Tarzán?"

Tarzán, a dealer who operates on horseback up in the hills, was recently released from prison in Tijuana after doing time for stabbing his brother-in-law in the ass for cheating on his sister.

Scoring in the Baja is much more Third World than working the streets of Harlem or D.C.

"Sure," I say. "I'll check out Tarzán first."

Richard tosses me the keys and tells me to go easy on his blue BMW sedan.

I walk out to the garage in front of the house, start the car and navigate the narrow cobblestone streets of the little seaside development in which we live. I drive out the front gate and up a steep dirt path to the toll road between Tijuana and Ensenada.

I floor it when I hit the highway.

The sun is out, but it's been raining for days, turning all but the paved roads—of which there are a limited number—into foul rivers of mud. This is one of the reasons for trying to find Tarzán. The mud trail to his place is likely to be more passable than some of the others.

The sun is blazing down as I drive up to Tarzán's house, hitting the dirt roads up into the hills as soon as I get to Rosarito Beach. I put a Ramones cassette in the BMW's tape deck and turn the volume up as high as it will go, buoyed by the knowledge that I should feel great within the hour.

The BMW fishtails through the mud with *Rockaway Beach* blasting from the speakers.

The car looks like it's been on safari by the time I get to Tarzán's place. I find him, wearing jeans, cowboy hat and boots, astride his horse on the muddy path in front of his house.

He looks down at me and considers my mud-splattered jeans and mud-caked sneakers.

"*Buenos tardes,*" I say.

"*Buenos tardes,*" he says.

I ask for six curas and give him sixty dollars.

Tarzán hands over the dope. I ask if he has any cocaine. He does. I buy ten dollars worth, or a half-gram, coke being a wonderful bargain in the Baja thanks to the fact that it became a major drug gateway to the U.S. after the Tijuana cartels took over from the Colombians.

I'm going to get back in the mud-encrusted BMW and drive back to the house as fast as I can, but I feel like getting high immediately.

"You mind if I get high before I leave?" I say, using hand gestures to indicate that I want to shoot up.

"*Donde?*" Tarzán says.

"In the car?"

"No. Somebody see, is very bad."

"Do you have someplace I can go?"

He toys with his gray mustache and points to a crumbling wooden shack outside of which dozens of chickens are milling and clucking.

It is Tarzán's chicken coop.

I am not a chicken person. They are foul, dirty, smelly, ill-tempered creatures that deserved to be turned into McNuggets and be eaten by someone other than me.

It is the best I'm going to do, however, since Tarzán clearly doesn't want a gringo shooting dope in a car parked outside his house.

I want to shoot up a speedball and if Tarzán's chicken coop is the only refuge available, the chicken coop it shall be. I will not let a bunch of scummy Mexican chickens come between drugs and me.

"Cool," I say to Tarzán. "*Gracias.*"

"*De nada,*" he says. "Be careful the chicken. No hurt."

"No problem," I say.

I walk to the chicken coop, wiping sweat from my forehead. The temperature is in the eighties and as I get closer to the coop, the nauseating stench of chicken shit fills my nostrils. I beat down the urge to puke, plowing ahead like a man who will not be denied, watching the clucking chickens, clearly unhappy with an intruder in their feathery and awful midst, scatter as I approach.

I duck and go through the low doorway.

Fuck almighty.

It's nearly a hundred degrees inside and hellish. The stench is overpowering. The chickens, disturbed by my presence, are clucking manically.

Screw them.

I sit down on a wooden crate and start preparing the coke and dope I'm going to shoot as I stifle an overwhelming wave of nausea.

I'm dripping in sweat. Feathers are flying. Chickens are approaching me, trying to peck my legs.

"Get out of here," I growl. "Go away! Shoo!"

The chickens ignore me.

"*Andalé*!" I yell, kicking at them. "*Andalé*!"

If it's true that your surroundings don't matter when you're trying to get off, that the only important thing is the drug, Tarzán's chicken shack in the hills proves the point beyond a shadow of a doubt.

I've done drugs in shooting galleries, crack houses, abandoned buildings, million dollar homes, apartments, condos, offices, government buildings, department stores, hotel rooms, youth hostels, rooming houses, doorways, bathrooms, vacant lots, parking lots, parked cars, moving vehicles, public toilets, alleys, parks, stairwells, elevators, airplane bathrooms, train restrooms, subway trains, buses, taxis, dingy basements, bars, clubs, cafés, restaurants, theaters, museums, amusement parks, arenas and stadiums.

But never in a chicken coop.

It doesn't matter. I could be in the middle of a crocodile farm or a serpentarium, for all I care. The only important thing is the syringe with the mega-speedball I'm about to do. A solid shot of fire and ice.

I stick the needle in my arm, find a willing vein and shoot up.

Yes.

Bells ring. A little cash register in my mind starts going cha-ching, cha-ching, cha-ching. A hundred slot machines in Vegas all hit the jackpot at once.

That's what I'm talking about—the Music of the Spheres.

Fuck the chickens.

I feel like the King of the Baja. Like Frank Fucking Perdue with a major attitude.

So what if the glory is all in my mind because, in reality, I'm crouching in chicken shit and my sneakers are encrusted with droppings, mud and feathers?

I stand up and brush myself off, kicking at the chickens near my feet.

"Kiss my ass," I mutter to a particularly aggressive rooster.

Time to go before I pass out, puke or do violence to Tarzán's chickens.

I gather my gear and march out of the chicken coop as though I'm exiting the Plaza Hotel with a beautiful model at my side and climbing into my Rolls.

Tarzán is still sitting on his horse. I nod, thank him and tell him I'll see him soon.

After firing up a righteous speedball, the drive back down the hill through the mud is like an amusement park ride thanks to the one-two punch of the dope and coke. The car fishtails and skids up and down the hills. When I hit the Toll Road and get north of Rosarito, I floor it and blaze back to our place on the Pacific at 90 MPH.

Right now, with all my cares erased by a speedball and the bright February afternoon sun, the Baja is a very cool place indeed.

About the Rain

The leaden, pewter clouds are so loaded with ocean moisture that every time they explode into another torrential, wind driven downpour, it feels like the rain will never end.

The pounding, drenching Pacific rains go on hour after hour.

Day in. Day out.

I watch storm after storm rolling in on the satellite photos on the San Diego TV weather reports and cringe.

Outside, the Pacific is as angry and gray as I am despondent and blue.

I lay on my back on the mattress of my second floor bedroom loft, sensing the onset of dope withdrawal—chills, cold sweat and runny nose—and stare at the ceiling.

Rainwater leaking through the roof is dripping into a bucket a couple of feet from my head. Another leak is plop-plop-plopping into a pot near my feet. A glass pitcher is filling slowly near the door.

Every pot, pan and container in the house has been pressed into service.

The house leaks like a sieve.

Among the things you leave behind when you say adios to *Los Estados Unidos* at the San Ysidro border crossing at Tijuana are roofs that keep out the rain.

Everything leaks down here in *Meh-Hee-Coh*, from expensive homes owned by gringos to the shacks of dirt-poor Mexican laborers.

Dripping water is as constant a background noise as pounding surf.

The first two words I added to my minuscule Spanish vocabulary when I arrived in Mexico were *cura*, which is what they call the single doses of black tar heroin that saturate the local drug marketplace, and *lluvia*, which means rain.

Even worse than the incessant lluvia is the fact that it turns large parts of the landscape to oozing brown liquid which, in turn, messes mightily with my ability to get a cura when I want/need one.

The locals joke that Rosarito has two names:

Rosa*lodo*, because everything turns to mud during the winter rains.

And, Rosa*polvo*, because choking dust fills the air when things dry out.

The *polvo* is a pain in the ass, coating everything in a fine earth brown powder, but I live in dread of the *lluvia* because of the *lodo.*

Lodo is the enemy.

Many local roads, other than the highway between Tijuana and Cabo San Lucas and other significant ones, are unpaved. Much of the reliable supply of dope, on the other hand, emanates from the dealers who live up in the hills above town. The dope comes from a handful of individuals and families that pay off the cops and are allowed to sell dope to local gringos by the Mexican authorities. Unfortunately, the hills are inaccessible in a normal vehicle once the roads become steep trails of mud and muck.

When the sky opens up, getting dope becomes an infinitely trickier task, made more difficult by shortages in money that prevent stockpiling, not that a stockpile of dope can ever last as long as intended.

And so, life reduces to a simple equation:

Lluvia = *Lodo* = *No Curas* = Great Unhappiness.

On some days when the roads turn to slop, Richard and I score *curas* in Rosarito Beach from a small-time local dealer who lives in a relatively paved part of town that caters to tourists. Mostly, however, the rain means that I'll be damp, miserable and dope sick, and that I'll spend the day glumly listening to depressing music, watching pelicans struggling to fly in the gale force winds coming off the Pacific and feeling nauseous. All to the tormenting background sound of water *plop-plop-plopping* through the roof into our collection of pots, pans and pails.

This is not the *Paradiso Mexicano* I had in mind when I decided to relocate to the Baja California.

I get up and go downstairs.

Richard is sitting in front of the fireplace, keeping warm and dry and reading a magazine.

"What do you want to do?" I say. "I'm getting sick."

We're supposed to be writing a novel together. This is why I put nearly everything I own that I haven't already sold to buy dope into storage and moved to the Baja from DC. But, mostly, we hang out and shoot and smoke Mexican black tar dope.

"I'm not driving to Rosarito," Richard says, knowing that our local drug transactions are simpler when he does the transacting because whereas I'm completely *gringo*, he has Mexican roots, speaks Spanish and has been hanging out here since he was a child.

Richard belongs. I do not.

"Why not?" I say.

"Have you looked outside?"

"I want to get some dope."

"There's none around."

"Aren't you starting to feel like shit?"

"I'll be okay."

"Come on. Maybe Baby has some."

Baby, so-called, is our dope contact in Rosarito Beach. He lives in a little pink cinder block house with his mother a couple of blocks from the beach and a big club called Papas & Beer.

"I doubt it," Richard says, turning his attention back to the magazine. "Last time we saw baby he asked us to get *him* some."

"Come on. I feel like shit."

"We agreed not to get dope every day."

Richard and I resolve *every day* to moderate our dope intake and, every day, I whine and complain enough to erode this resolve and we end up making a dope run into Rosarito or up to La Gloria, a rundown, poor village in the hills above town.

Because of the rain, our last shopping trip for drugs was several days ago. We carefully rationed the dope, but the last of it went early this morning.

And, now, desperation is taking hold in a major way.

"We're not doing dope every day," I say. "We've done it four days in a row. Before that, we didn't do it for three."

"I don't want to get strung out," Richard says.

"We *are* strung out."

"We can't afford to get loaded every day."

"It's *my* money."

I remind Richard that we exist on the paycheck I am still drawing from the magazine in Washington for which I ostensibly work, money I am receiving to write articles from Mexico and Southern California that I'm not writing.

It is a great gig, but unlikely to last much longer.

"Don't tell me how to spend my money," I continue.

"It's my house."

"Oh, right. I forgot. This is your *castle*."

"*What* did you say?"

Increasingly, and especially when we're under dope-caused duress, Richard and I bicker and curse each other out like an estranged couple.

"Fuck you and your *castle*," I say.

I gesture around the vast and empty living room. After Richard's mother passed away suddenly in the house several years ago, his family emptied the place out, intending to sell it until Richard decided to move in. The furniture and accessories in the living room consist of a workstation for his Mac, 1,000 CDs I shipped from Washington, a boom box, several chairs belonging to the outside deck and a dining table with chairs.

Richard takes the car keys from his pocket, throws them at me, and shouts, "Take the car, motherfucker! Get out of here! Go do what you want!"

"Thank you," I say, triumphant. "You want any dope?"

"If you don't like the house, leave."

"I love the house. You know that. I'm sorry. Do you want any dope?"

"If you find some."

"I'll drive to La Gloria if I have to."

"Don't take the car off the paved road. Park at the grocery store in La Gloria and walk."

There is, at least, a paved road that runs into the middle of La Gloria, from which, the dope dealers' houses are a good hike through the Baja mud.

I drive south down the toll road from Tijuana in the torrential rain toward Rosarito, glancing occasionally to the right at the angry Pacific and the dark canopy of clouds.

My first stop in Rosarito Beach, which has a paved main drag and many unpaved side streets, is Baby's place. He is sitting at his kitchen table surrounded by pots and pans to catch the rain dribbling through the roof.

I ask if he has any curas.

He looks miserable and says that he hasn't had any in two days and, as far as he knows, a lot of the dealers in the hills are out too. People are knocking on the door every fifteen minutes. Nobody has anything.

"What about Israel and Ishmael?" I say, referring to a family of Biblically named dope dealers who supply most of the gringos in Rosarito and environs with Mexican tar, as long as their payoffs to the various police agencies—local, state and federal—remain current.

Baby shrugs and says, "You know I no go there."

He has a long running dispute with Israel, Ishmael and Family.

I walk back through the Mexican mud and rain to Richard's old BMW sedan, and head up into the hills on a narrow, curvy and rain-slicked—but paved—road pockmarked with humongous potholes.

Fifteen minutes later, it is pouring harder than ever and I pull into the mud in front of the small grocery store in La Gloria just up the road from a Pemex gas station and down the road from the local police station.

Israel's and Ishmael's house is across the road, about a quarter mile up a steep slope of mud.

I get out of the car, pull up the hood on my jacket in a futile attempt to keep dry and trudge across the road through the cold February rain.

A few hundred yards up the hill, I sink into six inches of mud. It oozes through and under my jeans and into my shoes. I long to score in a place where I don't run the risk of being buried in a mudslide and not being found until an archeologist excavates me in 1,500 years.

Homo Gringodopefiendicus.

I curse out loud and continue marching up the steep hill through the downpour, hoping that I don't fall face first into the brown Baja California slime.

I look like a mud wrestler when I reach the house. Israel's wife answers the door.

She looks at me and invites me in.

"I am surprise you come," she says.

"I know," I say. "A lot of *lluvia* and *lodo*."

"Where is *Ree*-Shard?"

"He doesn't want to come out. I come for him."

"Is okay."

"You have *curas*?"

"*Si.* How *mush* you *wan*?"

"Eight. *Ocho*."

I'll buy eight, tell Richard I got four and keep the extra dope for myself.

"You *way* here," she says.

She walks into another room. I stand near the door, watching rain dripping from a dozen different leaks in the roof into pots, pans and buckets.

She returns with eight deep brown *curas* of Mexican tar encased in Saran Wrap and foil. I give her eighty dollars.

A minute later, I'm sliding back down the steep hill through the mudflow.

I am drenched to the bone and splattered with mud, but I have dope in my pocket and I know that, eventually, the rain has to stop.

*

I am coming to the realization that my friend Richard does not do well banging cocaine or firing up speedballs.

This profound revelation, as such, has come to me based upon Richard's increasingly bizarre behavior since we hit the hills near Rosarito Beach after the arrival of my paycheck from Washington. The fact that I'm getting *paid* to do what I'm doing—which is to smoke weed, shoot dope and sit on a balcony overlooking the gray-green sea and pounding surf while nodding out to the Cure and Joy Division—is an astounding thing.

It is as though I've been awarded a fellowship to research my dissertation on consuming narcotics in Mexico. Such is life in Richard's gorgeous cliff top oceanfront home, a short distance south of Tijuana.

A few days after the official beginning of spring, we return from the hills near town with a boatload of drugs and a seventeen-year-old local Mexican drug addict whom we acquire in the northern part of Rosarito Beach—a town famous for being the site of the filming of *Titanic* and for its spring break action.

We now have cocaine as well as Mexican Mud heroin. Enrique, the local junkie, is a grungy-looking kid with stringy black hair, darting deep brown eyes and a wispy teenaged John Waters mustache. Enrique has linked us to the local dealer with mucho cocaine, which he euphemistically refers to as *El Coche Blanco* (as opposed to *El Coche Negro*, for the tar heroin).

Enrique has also volunteered to do household chores in return for drugs. Even though Richard's house has almost no furniture—the ultimate in oceanfront junkie minimalism, who wants to spend money on furniture when you need every peso you can get your hands on for dope, cigarettes, rice, beans and tortillas?—it is great to have someone around to sweep, do laundry and take care of other tasks that fall by the wayside when Richard and I are off in our little drug induced la-la lands for days at a time.

Since the drug dollar goes further in *Meh-hee-Co* than it does in San Diego or L.A., because of the overhead added by having to transport the shit north of the border, we are able to spend much more time in the Land of Nod than we would in *Los Estados Unidos.*

If more American dope fiends understood that Mexico is a nirvana of narcotics, the *Mexican government* would have to put up a wall along the border to protect the republic from the strung out gringo hordes.

The trouble, of course, with cheap Mexican smack is that you tend to become *very* strung out on very good dope. So, when my cash runs out between paychecks and Richard can't borrow more money from his father in San Diego, dope sickness of Biblical proportions sets in.

Now, the *Coche Blanco*, will add an unexpectedly wonderful patina of *mierda* to everything.

With the new coke supply, the world starts to revolve around doing a Mexican Speedball, ideally every 45-60 minutes:

One small rat turd size piece of Mexican Mud heroin. (Ten dollars per turd from any of a number of Rosarito dealers that safely sell to resident gringos because they pay the cops to allow them do so.)

+

Water. (Less than a penny a shot, from the big water cooler jugs of spring water that everybody has in their home, including a lot of Mexicans. Shooting up Mexican tap water is not recommended.)

+

One big fat line of cocaine mixed into the cooked up liquid of brown tar and water. (Twenty dollars a gram for some pretty good shit.)

=

An enchanting high that is like racing at 100 MPH in a velvet coach. (Priceless.)

Our days dissolve into vague and fuzzy periods of time that separate one intravenous shot of cocaine and heroin from another.

All would be okay except for the presence of Enrique, to whom I am supplying drugs and with whom I get into frequent nasty junkie arguments.

Drugs and household items begin disappearing, and Enrique is the culprit, although he defends himself vigorously, like any good junkie would, albeit in shattered English.

Enrique's career as our houseboy comes to an end after he absconds with a pair of Richard's sunglasses that hold some sentimental value.

I am sleeping the sleep of the dead one night when Richard bursts into my room and tells me to get dressed. I look up at him like he is crazy. He announces that intruders are outside—he has seen them with his very own eyes in front of the house.

I sit up.

Richard's circle of friends and associates in the Baja includes an assortment of regular people, businessmen, dope using ex-patriots, ex-pats hiding out in Mexico, dope dealers and workaday locals.

On and off, Richard messes with some unsavory types, particularly in our mutual pursuit of drugs on credit when I am between paychecks.

Recently, he has been disappearing for long periods of time, doing God knows what. These trips into the hills east of Rosarito Beach and up to Tijuana and environs could be related to whoever is outside or whoever Richard is paranoid about, that he imagines is outside.

It is entirely possible that any of a number of individuals could be outside. These fears that there are people wanting to do harm upon our persons is one of the things that is making life in *Meh-hee-coh* a little edgy. Way edgier than I'd ever envisioned when I moved south of the border so Richard and I could write a novel.

We're not writing one, although, I may be living one.

"Are you kidding?" I say.

"No," Richard says.

"Are you seeing things?"

"I'm serious. There are people outside."

Richard has been working on obtaining guns for the house, insisting that we need them for our safety, but none have yet materialized.

What are we supposed to do, however, if there are really people outside?

We don't even have a barking dog. The closest thing is an insanely loud parrot that belongs to the gay couple next door.

The truth is that the little gated development in which we live is virtually deserted this time of year. On the ocean side of the house, the sound of the crashing surf is so loud, especially at high tide, that you could fire a gun and it would be barely audible.

It is not only high tide, but a full moon high tide tonight.

I put on jeans, grab a jacket and follow Richard downstairs. He goes to the fireplace and grabs several heavy, sharp tools—indispensable for getting a fire going, less useful if you need to shoot someone.

"What are we supposed to do with these?" I ask.

"We can pretend we have guns."

Pretend we have guns? What if they *have* guns? Won't *pretending* we have guns encourage them to use the real guns they possess?

Am I about to die in some awful Mexican violence that belongs in an indie movie about a druggy lifestyle and violent death in *Meh-hee-coh*?

"Oh Christ," I said. "Why don't we call the police?"

"This is Mexico. You don't call the police here."

I follow Richard outside.

He screams, "We're here motherfuckers and we have guns! Come near us and we'll blow your fucking brains out!"

"There's two of us," I add bravely. "You fucking pricks."

Both of us brandish the fireplace tools like they will be of use if we are confronted by Tijuana drug cartel thugs with heavy artillery.

"Assholes!" Richard yells.

We walk around the brick patio in front of the house. I don't see or hear anything, and conclude that we are chasing a figment of Richard's imagination.

Paranoid delusions, I believe a working mental health professional would call them.

"We've got to check out back," Richard says.

"Why?"

"Maybe they went to the beach."

We walk around the side of the house. A full moon is hanging above the Pacific, casting a long beam of light on the surface of the water. We walk around back. The only thing that is evident is the sound of waves crashing thunderously on the rocks.

Richard goes down the long, winding staircase, several stories down to the beach. I stand guard at the top.

I watch him prowling around for a few minutes, illuminated by the moonlight.

When he returns, he concedes that no one is there. I grumble as we return to the house, bickering with Richard about whether we are surrounded by vengeful Mexicans that intend to do us harm or whether, perhaps, he had seen something and mistaken it for angry locals.

We go back around the house and go inside, walking out to the balcony to survey the scene again. There is the full moon, crashing surf, the flashing beacon of the lighthouse on Coronado Island. Otherwise, nothing.

"Richard, there's nothing," I say.

"Let's check out front again."

"Why?"

"I know I saw something."

We go through the house again, and out the front door.

It is a cold night. I am wearing an army jacket and jeans, but no shirt.

We walk to the wall around the front patio. Richard peers over it at the vacant land next to the house.

"There," he whispers, pointing at the empty landscape.

I see nothing other than shrubs and weeds.

"Where?" I say.

"Over there."

He gestures toward some vegetation.

I see bushes and shadows and say so.

Richard curses and says that I must be blind. Don't I see them?

"We know you're out there, motherfuckers!" he hollers. "Get the fuck out of here! More people are coming!"

Ten minutes of more of this kind of thing pass.

"Richard, I don't think anything is out there but rats," I finally say. "Maybe we scared the guys away."

"Maybe. I'm going to make sure we get guns as soon as we can."

"Yeah. We should have guns."

I go upstairs, get back in bed and fall dead asleep. An hour later, Richard is shaking me awake again.

"They're out there," he says. "Meet me downstairs."

"Wha?"

"Get downstairs."

He leaves. I must fall asleep within a minute of his departure.

When I wake up, the sun is shining and Richard is downstairs cursing and demanding that I come down.

I descend the stairs while trying to shake off the cobwebs of a deep sleep.

"You asshole," he says.

"Why are you cursing at me?"

"You left me out there."

"What are you talking about?"

"They were out there and you never came down."

It takes me a moment to remember that he had woken me up again and asked me to come downstairs.

"Jesus, I must have fallen asleep," I say. "I'm sorry."

"It's great that you're sorry, but they could have killed me. You let me down."

"What happened?"

Richard explains that when he went back outside he was trapped in the garage while the intruders stalked around outside. Turns out, he was in the garage until dawn.

"You screwed me," he says.

"I did no such thing. I fell asleep."

"I could've been killed."

"Nobody was out there."

Richard grabs the car keys from the counter, announces that he's driving into Rosarito and storms off.

I go out to the balcony and bask in the early morning Baja California sun, wondering if it's time to return home and celebrate spring in Washington.

WASHINGTON D.C.

It is three thirty in the morning. I am sitting on a skuzzy, disintegrating sofa in a crack house in a not very nice neighborhood in Washington, D.C.

I pick absentmindedly at bits of sofa stuffing, pull clumps from a cushion and drop them on the floor.

I should be in bed. In fact, a few hours ago, I *was* in bed because I've got to interview a Congressman from New York at 10:30, which is less than eight hours from now.

That was before Haddad—a Palestinian limo driver and crackhead whose acquaintance I made recently—knocked on my door a little after one in the morning.

I am trying to take a vacation from drugs, especially cocaine-type drugs that tend to lead to multi-day binges and interfere with the smooth and orderly progression of life. Haddad's arrival, however, reignites my interest in them.

He is Pavlov. I am the dog. I drool uncontrollably. A two-day vacation from drugs is long enough.

Hence, the crack house.

I generally avoid crack houses, not so much because they have an image problem, but because they truly suck.

Poster children for the ravages of hard core drug abuse are all around me.

A thin girl with stringy, dirty blonde hair, she's maybe eighteen, offers to blow me in return for a rock. She's the kind of girl who looks like she was cute before she started giving guys blowjobs for hits of crack. Now, she's just very young and very strung out and in need of a couple of years in locked-down rehab with a serious security perimeter fence.

Even if I'm interested in her offer, it wouldn't matter. I'm almost out of drugs and so is the crack house. There is nothing that any woman could offer me to make me part with my last crumbs of drugs in what may be the only crack house in the District of Columbia that has no crack.

The drugs are supposed to be here soon.

In the meantime, the crack house has the air of an especially tragic funeral. Human warmth and animation diminish or increase in direct relation to the size of the drug stash.

Haddad is scrutinizing the top of a table looking for stray crumbs of crack that might have escaped vaporization in his stem.

A black chick is down on her hands and knees examining the filthy floor for the same thing.

I'm trying to de-stuff the sofa.

The young blonde again says she'll trade sex for a hit of rock, this time offering to do the "whole deal" in the bathroom for one miserable hit.

I tell her that I'd *give* her a hit. We don't have to have sex. If I had enough rock for two people. Which I don't.

"I know you've fucking got some," she says.

She retreats to the opposite side of the room—which is populated with an assortment of maniacally desperate people except for the one or two who still have some drugs left and would not part with it if you put a gun to their heads—and starts to sulk.

The proprietor of the crack house is marching around with a sawed-off shotgun at his side like an especially maniacal bouncer.

Who cares? The only question with any meaning is: Where's the rock?

I look around. A chestnut colored mutt is wandering the room looking no happier than the human inhabitants. My limo driver buddy is now slumped in a chair rubbing his forehead, looking like he wants to die. Two black girls, probably no more than thirty, both of them missing most of their front teeth, are staring sullenly at the floor. Another guy who is either in his sixties or a very old forty-five and living proof of the wondrous effects of serious drugs, keeps coming in and out of the house. Each entry and exit prompts a trip to the door by our host with the shotgun.

Our host calls himself T-Bone.

Just like the steak.

Two kids are running around the place. One's an infant who is crawling around the floor. The other is six or seven. I'm not sure if they're T-Bone's kids or someone else's.

The dog pisses on the floor. T-Bone kicks the mutt, who yelps and runs into the other room. He orders the six-year-old to clean up the dog piss.

The kid cleans. The dog yelps.

I stare at the floor and wonder what I'm doing here and why I don't call child protective services and the ASPCA. But I know why. Because I'm part of the problem and not the solution, is why.

Where's the rock?

I would leave if I could, but I can't. We drove over in my Palestinian buddy's Lincoln Towncar, but the Towncar isn't here any more. Haddad gave it to a couple of teenagers for twenty dollars worth of rock. They said they'd be back in fifteen minutes. That was two hours ago. They're probably halfway to New York by now.

Leaving on foot would be suicidal. A white guy walking down the street in this neighborhood at four in the morning would not last long. I've already tried to snag a cab. Ten minutes on the street waiting and getting sized up by a couple of guys with hungry eyes sent me back to the crack house.

Whether this says more about the neighborhood or me, I don't know. I have cursed and screamed at my Palestinian friend and suggested the next time his dumb ass shows up at my apartment building, I'm calling the cops.

I can blame him all I want, but a fact is a fact and it's time to face facts. This is my fault too. You get into fucked up situations like this one when you hang out in the sub-basements of the drug world.

I check my watch.

Shit. It's four thirty.

The Washington Metro isn't far, but it stops at midnight and won't start running again until five-thirty. By then, the sun will be up and it will be safe to leave.

I will have a couple of hours to decompress, shower and shave. The congressman will never know that a crack- and heroin-crazed reporter is sitting across the desk from him.

What he doesn't know won't hurt him.

We're supposed to talk about illegal immigration. Better to chat about Mexicans walking, swimming, running and crawling across our southern frontier than, say, *drug policy.*

Still, I'm going to have to get my hands on some drugs if I stand any chance of making it through the day.

I point at Haddad.

"This is your fault," I say.

"They say they take car ten minute," he says, in heavily accented English.

"How could you give away the car for a three-dollar hit?"

"Was not tree dollar. Was twenty dollar. Ten minute with car. Good deal."

"Yeah, great deal."

"What I do about car? I must *eggsplain* car."

"That's your problem," I say.

"I am fuck without car," he groans, no doubt imagining the teen gangsters using his Towncar to cruise for crack whores in Washington Heights or having it deconstructed at a chop shop in Hunt's Point.

I couldn't care less about the car, except that its absence has stranded me in this crack-less hell hole until sunrise. I hope they drive it into the East River. It would serve Haddad's dumb ass right.

I stare at the floor for a long time.

Someone knocks on the door. Our host answers, shotgun drawn. A guy comes in and hands him a baggie full of pre-packaged crack.

"You *zee*," Haddad says. "I tell you rock come."

The room goes from miserable and quiet to loud and happy as T-Bone makes the rounds selling rock from the baggie.

When he reaches me, I hand him sixty dollars and get a dozen of tiny plastic ziplock bags in return. I pack my stem and do a quick hit, immediately going from feeling dead to undead, and pocket the rest.

I can see the outlines of weak light around the curtains and shades.

I get up. I ask our host to unlock the door. He walks me to the door with his shotgun. He is either protecting me or getting ready to shoot me as I leave.

I step outside. It is already warm and profoundly humid.

Daylight has returned.

I check my watch. It's nearly five-thirty.

I have drugs in my pocket. The Metro will be running in a few minutes.

I can finally go home and get my shit together for another day.

North of the Border

My buddy Richard's in town and so is the shit he's brought with him in large quantity from San Diego. Richard has relocated to Mexico while he figures out what to do with the rest of his life.

The process is very much touch-and-go.

I've been back home in D.C. for only four weeks after spending the previous six months living at Richard's place in the Baja California.

I went to Mexico to get away from dope and write a novel with Richard about a reverse immigration future when gringos are flooding Mexico from California. The only problem being that we wrote one 1,500-word short story loosely based on an antique dealing junkie chick from L.A. named Lauren.

It was a good short story, especially in the way it succinctly captured the foul underbelly of gringo junkie life south of the border. But the rest of the trip turned into a strung-out nightmare of high-octane black tar heroin and high-quality cocaine.

The Baja California is not a good place to which to repair if you are trying to stop using drugs.

Richard and I were not on the best of terms when I fled the Baja for my old life back in D.C. because the problems in Mexico were growing in number and variety.

Money problems.

Drug dealer problems.

Domestic problems.

Women problems.

No more credit at the bar down the road problems.

Cocaine-induced psychosis (his, not mine) problems.

My ex-, upon learning of the ugly domestic scene in the Baja, invited me to crash at her place.

Now, however, with Richard in D.C., staying at a hotel a few blocks from Dupont Circle, we're best friends again.

Like brothers.

This is because of the shit.

Shit is the tie that binds.

Somebody smuggled the shit—Mexican black tar heroin—north through the border at Tijuana for him. Richard flew it to D.C. from San Diego.

"I'm here," Richard announces on the phone.

I'm sitting at my desk in the newsroom at the magazine where I work.

"Everything's cool, right?" I say.

"Yeah, everything's fine," he says.

"Good. How's the hotel?"

"It's okay. It's a nice big room with a good view of the neighborhood. It should be comfortable. I feel a lot better about things than the last time I was here."

The last time Richard was in town he was trying to kick dope. I'm actually surprised he can stand to set foot in D.C. again. Spending three days in a cold sweat, throwing up and running back and forth to the toilet is the kind of thing that can turn you against a place big time.

"You want me to drop by?" I say.

I have a 5,000-word story due tomorrow and the entire office is moving to new digs in a few days, but the details of life can wait.

"Yeah," he says. "Whenever."

"Good," I say. "I'll be right there. It's a fifteen minute walk from here."

I take a cab and get there in five.

When I get to the hotel, Richard and I hug like brothers.

All of the bad blood of Mexico is forgotten.

"So," I say. "How's the dope?"

"I've got it," he says.

"How much did you bring?"

"A couple of ounces."

"Cool."

Super fucking cool, in fact.

Two ounces of tar. A man can go into a nod for quite a few days on that.

Too bad I can't afford to buy it all and that it doesn't belong to Richard either. The dope is north of the border on consignment.

"It was easy," Richard says. "Paco had some guys bring it over. All I had to do was pick it up in San Diego."

Paco is Richard's disreputable Tijuana contact, a minor member of a fairly significant dope operation. Paco provided the dope and had it transported via mule to San Diego. It's a lot of trouble to go to for a couple of ounces of dope, but a new market is a new market.

And the Nation's Capital is clearly a new market for Mexican Black Tar. We should have a Harlem-style dope line running from the entrance of the hotel where he's staying right down New Hampshire Avenue to Dupont Circle. The white powder dope they sell in D.C. is baby laxative compared to Mexican shit.

"Can I get a shot?" I say. "I'm dying for it. Everything here is total shit by comparison."

"You have money?" Richard says.

"What?"

"Do you have any money?"

"You're going to make me *pay* for it?"

"It isn't my shit."

"After we spent all *my* money in Mexico on drugs? You won't give me a hit?"

"I told you, it isn't mine to give."

"So? It's one hit. Who's going to miss it?"

"Fine," Richard says. "No problem. You can have a hit."

"Thank you."

He goes into the bedroom. I hear him rummaging. He returns with something that looks like a goopy black golf ball on steroids wrapped in aluminum foil.

"You want any more of this shit," he says. "You're going to have to pay for it. I'm not kidding."

"I can't believe this."

"The shit isn't mine. Okay?"

"What about all the dope I bought for us in Mexico?" I say.

"This is a business deal."

"You're treating me like a street corner drug dealer."

As this exchange is going on, he's cutting dope from the golf ball for me, making a small slice of sticky black tar that we called a *cura*—cure—in Mexico.

That's because it's the *cure* for everything that ails you until the cure, itself, starts ailing you. At which point, you're fucked.

There's something warm and comforting about sitting in a hotel room in Dupont Circle in Washington waiting to do a *cura.*

Richard gives me the *cura.* I turn to the task of melting it down in a teaspoon of water and drawing it into a syringe through a small piece of filter from one of my Marlboros. Richard turns on the TV. The remake of *The Getaway* is on TV.

I shoot up to Kim Basinger and settle back on the couch, enjoying the kind of rush I haven't felt in weeks. I came back from Mexico with a Jones the size of Texas. There's no way to keep it happy with D.C. dope.

Now, all that's changed.

"Have you called anybody?" Richard says.

"No, not yet," I say. "They know you're coming. I figured I'd wait until you got here."

"Well, I'm here. Why don't we see what kind of business we can drum up?"

What kind of business *we* can drum up?

"Sure," I say. "But what am I going to get out of this?"

"I don't believe you."

"What?"

"How can you talk to me that way?" he says.

"I'm sorry, but I don't want to get screwed."

"You think *I'm* going to *screw* you?"

Richard's eyes narrow.

"I didn't mean it that way," I say.

"You won't get *screwed*," he says. "Don't worry."

"Well, then, can I have another hit?"

"Yeah, but only one more. I told you it's Paco's shit."

"Jesus Christ," I say. "I'll pay for my fucking dope, okay?"

"We'll work something out after we sell some. Why don't you make some calls?"

"Yeah, okay," I say.

Richard hands me another *cura*. I cook it up.

Phone calls? No problem. There's work to be done and shit to be moved.

Summer ABC's

Summer has landed on the Nation's Capital with a stifling and inhuman thud. Outside, the temperature is in the upper nineties and the humidity is stuck near an oppressive and ungodly 100 percent. The "heat index" says something like One Oh Five or One Ten. Making the transition from air conditioning to the great outdoors is like stepping into an overheated sauna run by someone who continually overheats rocks upon which vaporize vast quantities of water.

There is, of course, always the option of the rooftop pool of my Dupont Circle apartment building, but I've abandoned sunbathing due to general fears of UV radiation, the thinning ozone layer and carcinomas, not to mention the track marks and bruises on my arms from shooting dope.

In the days before I perfected the art of turning myself into a human pincushion, (i.e., last summer) there was only the stray red dot or welt and the occasional bruise where a shot of dope "missed," depositing heroin and miscellaneous chemicals, both benign and not, into flesh rather than a vein.

No longer.

My right arm is marked by a nasty red line of needle marks that approximates the Northeast rail corridor between Washington and New York City in shape, even down to clusters of puncture marks along my long suffering veins that could stand in for Baltimore, Wilmington and Philadelphia.

While the stubborn abscess in the crook of my right arm is finally healing after months of gross nastiness, taking the elevator up to the roof and jumping in the pool wearing a long sleeve shirt would only make me stand out, particularly among my Speedo clad gay neighbors.

Ah, yes, summer in Dupont Circle as a downwardly mobile young professional junkie.

While no time of year is a particularly good one to be hideously strung out on dope and ceaselessly craving crack, the gurgling and irritable bowels of a Washington summer are a particularly brutal time.

Particularly, the days when dope is scarce and withdrawal starts setting in before I can get straight. You haven't truly gotten a sense of life's nasty little underbelly until you know the feeling of getting dope sick on a blisteringly hot day and feeling bone chillingly cold in 100 degree heat.

And so, I hide in my Dupont Circle apartment and venture outside only to:

(A). Cop drugs, which I must do at least once a day.

(B). Buy cigarettes and "food" (Ring Dings, Yodels, Twinkies, Oreos, Etc.) at the Exxon station a block away.

(C). Make the occasional trip to the office, which I do with much less frequency than the former and only after I have copped, which means that the latter—which enables the former—doesn't happen at all on days when I don't hook up with dope until evening.

And…

(D). Sell off everything I own (particularly the CDs and books) or acquire things which are not mine to sell (laptops taken from the office in dead of night, shoulder bags full of expensive books destined for the local used book shop) to cover cash shortfalls and buy dope between paychecks. One of the reasons that God made used CD shops and used bookstores is to allow junkies who once enjoyed reading and listening to music the ability to raise cash without resorting to more brazen thievery, which I have also begun to do.

While (A) is the prevailing reality of summer, it is not guaranteed in the medium- to long-term sense since (A) will definitely be undermined by (C) and cannot be supported entirely by (D), which is most certainly the handwriting on the wall.

And, then, while indoors, there is….

(E). Fending off phone calls from credit card companies, which have taken to frequent and threatening phone calls since I ceased payment on my three Visa cards, two Mastercards and my American Express card, because a $100 a day dope habit cannot peacefully coexist with debt service, even in its most minimal form.

On this particular day, there have been two such calls, one handled by my answering machine and one, unfortunately, answered by me because I thought it was my drug dealer calling back.

"Hi, Robert, how are you?"

"Uh, fine."

"Robert, I'm calling about your outstanding balance, which as of today is 4,383 dollars and 68 cents."

"4,383 dollars and 68 cents. Right."

"As you know, you've missed the last two minimum monthly payments. One in the amount of $163 and the other in the amount of $171."

"I'm sorry about that."

"If there's a problem, we'd certainly like to know about it. But, as of now, Robert, your minimum payment is $509. When can we expect that?"

"I'm expecting a check within the next week. How about if I send you $100?"

"Our records show that you're employed full time. Is that still the case?"

"Yes, of course."

"I'm sorry, Robert, but we do need to ask for the full amount at this time. Anything less will result in your account being turned over to our collection department and it will be canceled."

"Collection? Canceled?"

"Yes."

"What do you mean?"

"You're going to be strictly cash and carry from here on out."

"Cash and carry? What?"

"You're not going to have credit cards anymore. You'll have a past due account and a bad credit rating. You will be cash only. For a long, long time."

"Fuck you, then."

"There's no reason to curse. If you just make the minimum payment…"

"I can't!!!"

"Sir, it's your obligation."

Yes, there are definitely ominous and dark clouds looming on the horizon come fall and, God forbid, winter. If summer is a crappy time to be a nearly penniless junkie, winter will be even worse.

And so, I'm spending entire days watching CNN Headline News while waiting for my dope man to come. I view so many repeated cycles of Headline News every day, day in and day out, that I may be one of the world's most superficially informed people. At the top and bottom of every hour I drool in a Pavlovian way, somehow associating the beginning and end of each newscast with getting my hands on a bag of dope, doing a shot and "getting straight," as they say. You no longer get particularly high when you're strung out so much as you ward off illness—chills, puking, cold sweat, apocalyptic diarrhea, etc. In fact, getting dope into your system and banishing the first signs of sickness—sneezing, runny nose and mild chills—is such a blessed relief that you actually get a giddy feeling knowing you won't be sick.

Every hour or so I page my dope dealer—who may be the only guy in town who delivers and does so on credit—and pray that he calls right back.

Sometimes he does.

Sometimes he doesn't.

Sometimes, I resort to Plan B, which is to contact a former boxer, and now crackhead dealer named John, AKA Smooth. Smooth will swing by with his car so that we can drive around frightening parts of D.C. looking for dope.

Smooth is not a good solution because the upfront price for his services is a portion of my dope and being nagged into buying some rock, whether I'm trying to save all my money for dope or not.

I try to be patient and not send too many 9-1-1's to Dealer *Numero Uno*, Jimmy, which is understood to be an emergency.

Since getting dope this summer is a constant emergency, the hourly 9-1-1 pages would cease to lose their impact. I generally wait until after sundown to send Jimmy a 9-1-1.

Today, Jimmy returns my calls at 7:30 in the evening, after I've gone to the Exxon station to pick up a pack of Marlboros, a Diet Coke and a package of Yodels.

The news is grim.

"Hey, Bob," he says. "I couldn't get back at you. I be travelin'."

My stomach sinks and I feel like hurling.

"Traveling?" I say.

"Me *an'* Sheri and Teisha be in *Norf* Carolina."

Sheri is Jimmy's certifiably insane or, at least, pathologically violent, wife. Teisha is his six-year-old daughter.

Several days ago, I sat in Jimmy's kitchen as Sheri argued with Jimmy on the phone, finally screaming, "All right, *muthafucka*, bring it on. I'm *strappin'* up and *comin'* to put a cap in *yo'* ass."

She grabbed a .22 from the cupboard behind some dishes, put the gun in her handbag and ran out the door, leaving me and Sammy, Jimmy's partner and occasional bill collector, sitting at the table debating whether Sheri would actually shoot Jimmy or would only threaten him with the gun, and whether we should call him to let him know that his wife was coming after him with a .22.

Sammy called Jimmy to tell him Sheri had a gun and wanted to put a cap in his ass.

"Did you say North Carolina, Jimmy?" I say.

"Yeah," he says. "Be nice here."

"You coming back tonight?"

He laughs and says, "Hell no. We *comin'* back *nex'* week. *Tu'day* or *Wehnsday.*"

"A week from now?"

"Yeah, me and Sheri *boaf* got big family here."

I shiver and break out in a cold sweat. What the hell am I going to do without Jimmy for a week? He's been my main supplier for nearly a year.

"*Gonna'* do me some *fishin'*," Jimmy says. "*Gonna'* eat me some barbecue. *Gonna'* have a big family reunion this *weeken'*."

I let out a *basso profondo* fart that indicates an impending case of the runs.

"Great," I say. "It's nice that you can spend time with your family."

"Sorry I couldn't help you *wif* some here-*oh*-on before I *lef.*"

"Yeah, that would've been nice."

"Trip came as a *suhprise*. We decided this *mornin'* and *jes lef fo Norf* Carolina."

"Right."

"Maybe Sammy can *hep* you out. Or Smooth."

I belch deeply, again beating back the urge to puke.

"Hey, no problem," I say. "I hope you enjoy yourselves.'

"See you *whens* we get back."

"Right. Enjoy."

I sit on the sofa, sweating despite the fact that the air conditioning is refrigerating the apartment. My bowels loosen. Since becoming familiar with the copping and using dope treadmill, I've learned that unpleasant things, or even very exciting things, can cause you to *shit yourself.*

Fuck.

This presents multiple problems:

(A). I was counting on Jimmy to front me more dope on credit because I'm not getting paid until Friday and my absolutely free checking account is absolutely empty.

(B). I now need to find Smooth, who will help me score, but in a time consuming and annoying way.

and

(C). Because of (A) and (B), I will now have to scour my rapidly diminishing shelves of music for several dozen CDs that I can sell at a used CD place before Smooth and I drive to the hellish D.C. street on which dope dealers are to be found today.

I sigh, concluding that the only option I have is:

(D). Calling Smooth.

I pick up the phone, dial Smooth's pager, punch in my number and wait for him to call back and make the summer night better.

*

The woman sitting in the living room of my Dupont Circle apartment in Washington with my dealer and friend Smooth is in her mid-twenties. She is African-American and has the look of a really hot female who is part way into a deep crack addiction; she is neither as good looking as she was before she started sucking on the Devil's Johnson nor as hideous as she will become after spending more quality time doing major suckee suckee.

She's holding up a variety of clothing for my inspection from a large bag she is carrying around, as though she has returned from a monstrous shopping excursion undertaken with a credit card from a makeover show.

Shirts.
Jeans.
Shorts.
Hats.
Ties.
Etc.

"This *Fee-your-you-see*," she says. "The real deal, *boo*."

She displays a green print shirt and points at the Fiorucci tag.

"That's nice," I say.

"I know it *nice*," says the woman, whose name is Shawanda. "And it look nice on you, you try it on."

"No thanks."

She pulls out a black shirt and displays it. "Prada," she says.

"Nice," I say.

"Shit be lookin' *good* on a big man like you. Try it. You like it, I give it to you for forty. Worth three hundred*fitty*. I *know* you got forty livin' in a crib like this."

She gestures around my apartment, which is an average place in a nondescript mid-sixties Washington apartment building. The furniture is multiple steps up the food chain from Ikea, and it is well equipped with electronic equipment. There are a large number of books and CDs on wall units in the living room, although significantly less of both than there once was. I am in the process of selling many of the books and CDs to subsidize my drug habit, but the collection—which was huge to start with—is still impressive.

"Where they from?" I say.

"*Fee-your-you-see an'* Prada," she says. "Just like it say. This ain't no knockoff shit. It be the *real* deal. Looks like your size too, baby."

I can see that it's Prada and Fiorucci. What I want to know is where the sister got the Prada and the *Fee-your-you-see* at and why she's like a walking designer boutique.

Smooth—who was a welterweight boxer back in the day—and is now a shiftless crackhead and dope addict who talks about what it was like when he was a boxer, looks at me and laughs. Smooth's real name is John. He says that "Smooth" is his name from his boxing days. People called him "Smooth" because he was such a *smooth* fighter. Other people say that he has acquired the nickname more recently, and that it is related to the fact that he bullshits and lies so effortlessly and smoothly.

Smooth shakes his head and says, "You can't beat them *kinda* prices."

"What size are the shirts?" I say.

"Most of '*em* mediums, *boo*," she says. "I got some large too. Ain't they *nice*?"

"No way," I say. I exhale a stream of smoke from a hit of rock I just smoked. Before coming back to my apartment and acquiring Shawanda from the streets of inner city Washington in the process, Smooth and I scored several bags of dope and about fifty bucks worth of rock.

"I'm an XXL or an XL," I say.

"You large at *bess*', baby," she says. "You keep *smokin'*, you *gonna'* be medium before you know it."

That's cool. I don't have a problem with weight loss.

Dope and rock help one shed massive poundage effortlessly. You can drop twenty or thirty pounds in a matter of weeks on a really good run without even breaking a sweat.

Normal people starve themselves to death or run like rodents on treadmills day in and day out to get that kind of result.

The hell with South Beach, low carbs and Dr. Atkins. Crack cocaine and heroin (Drs. White and Brown, respectively, or White and White, depending on the point of origin of the dope) are the real miracle diets. Guaranteed. (*Side effects may vary*).

Shawanda rummages in one of the bags again and lifts out a black shirt with a print of red, white and green ice pops on it. "This be *Mos-Chai-No*," she says. "Be a large. It say two hundred *fitty* on the tag. Hit me with 20 and it's yours."

Only Prada, Fiorucci and Moschino? No Dolce & Gabbana?

Shawanda and Smooth are sitting on my sofa. I'm sitting on a chair across from them. A guy in his sixties named Rufus, who has white hair and a less than average number of front teeth, is sitting on the floor leaning on my coffee table.

Rufus—who is probably somebody's *grandfather*—is saying, "Shit be good" repeatedly. Occasionally, he throws in, "Smooth, do me *anotha*' hit. I be good for it."

Rufus is stationary, which means I do not need to follow him around my apartment. The last time he came over with Smooth, a cheap souvenir watch I bought in Spain and several dollars in quarters I kept in a cup in my kitchen went missing.

I mix up a hit of dope in a teaspoon, suck the liquid into a syringe, tie off my right arm with a sock and shoot up in front of everybody like I'm drinking a shot of scotch.

At one time, I ran into the bathroom to shoot up, but I'm no long shy and, besides, leaving the premises unattended could result in petty theft on Rufus' part (Smooth won't steal from me and, as far as I know, Shawanda is only interested in big ticket items off the rack).

Shawanda holds up a woman's blouse and hands it to Smooth.

He examines it and says, "My wife would love this shit. How much you want for it?"

"That be Christian Dior, baby," she says.

"Give you a blast for it."

"Sold."

Shawanda smokes the big hit of rock Smooth gives her in exchange for the Dior blouse. I smoke another hit. Rufus watches us and begs for another hit. Smooth gives him a small piece.

"Shit be *fuckin'* all right," he says upon exhaling.

"Smooth," Shawanda says. "You take me down to Hecht's?"

She wants to go Hecht's, the big department store in downtown DC?

"I thought you banned from Hecht's," Smooth says.

"Nah, baby. I banned from Woodie's. I still *cool* at Hecht's."

Smooth looks at me and says, "Shawanda the best booster in DC. She incredible."

Really? I know good writers, kick ass photographers, successful lawyers, top-notch business people and, even, Class-A junkies and dope fiends. But Shawanda is the first *professional shoplifter* I've met.

I'm suitably impressed. "You make a living boosting?"

"Shit," she laughs. "I ain't even been *busted* that many times."

"You *wanna'* come?" Smooth asks me. "She can show you how."

I should be working. I have a story due tomorrow. I postponed the deadline on it last week when I was too stoned to bother writing by claiming a vague and debilitating illness to my editor. I've written, maybe, five paragraphs so far.

In fact, I should be writing my ass off right now, not hosting a crackhead convention in my apartment.

"Yeah, sure," I say. "Why not? We can stop for more rock later, right?"

"All you want," Smooth says.

It's two in the afternoon. Smooth drops Rufus off on U Street, then we head downtown so Shawanda can hit up Hecht's.

"They anything you need, Baby?" she asks me. "I give you a good price on it. Maybe we do a trade or *sumfin'*."

"I don't know," I say. "Maybe. We'll see."

We pull up in front of Hecht's. Shawanda gets out of the car and Smooth tells her we'll wait across the street.

We sit and wait. Fifteen minutes later, Shawanda walks out of the store. She runs across the street and jumps into the backseat.

"Go!" she says.

Smooth pulls out.

"Go!" she shouts. "Faster!"

We speed off down the street.

"What's up?" Smooth says.

"Security *asshole* be followin' me," she says. "Fuckin' *poh*-lice *muthafuckа'*."

She holds up a black shirt.

"It's extra large, baby, *jus'* like you want," she says. "Paul Smith."

It is a nice shirt. And it's in my color.

"How much you want for it?" I say.

"Twenty," she says. "It's worth a hundred *seveny*."

I reach into my pocket and give her a twenty. It's not like I stole the shirt. It's pre-stolen. I'm only buying it.

"I need a *blast*," Shawanda says. "Fuckin' *poh*-lice got me *trippin'*."

"*Less* get more rock," I tell Smooth.

He turns left through the downtown traffic, headed back to the dope spot.

NEW YORK

Black Friday

It is Black Friday, the day After Thanksgiving.

I have broken up with my girlfriend in Washington because of a post-Thanksgiving dinner altercation involving cooking (my lack thereof), unfulfilled clean up obligations (mine, again), my insistence on watching the Detroit Lions play football (a very bad thing, indeed) and my general anti-holiday attitude (profoundly negative).

Thanksgiving ended on a very sour note.

Specifically, with a drumstick thrown in my general direction (a permanent grease stain and slight indentation forever marking the impact site on the wall) and a loud "fuck you," also directed at me.

I am not decent holiday material, especially when my top priority is making a dope run up to New York City on the Friday after Thanksgiving.

For today, the breakup is blessing; it greatly simplifies the post-holiday dope run to New York. Were the girlfriend and I still together—which I suspect we will be again by next weekend—I would be forced to lie terribly about my whereabouts or, even worse, battle the Black Friday consumer masses with her to go Christmas shopping.

I grab a taxi on Seventh Avenue outside of Penn Station and tell the driver I need to go to East Harlem. He looks in the rearview, shakes his head and turns west in order to start the long ride north through the sluggish Midtown traffic.

Forty-five minutes later—after a horrendous uptown trip through horrible holiday congestion that makes me wish I'd taken the subway—I'm standing in the cold at the corner of East 123rd and Lexington, waving at my dope go-between Sal.

Sal is standing in front of the bodega where the old Dominican guy I buy much dope from—I only know him as "Papi" and he, in turn, calls me "Papi" too—does business. A fairly straight looking white chick with short brown hair is standing with him. Even from across the street, it's easy to tell she's pretty.

Sal sees me and screams, "Yo, Bobby! Yo!"

He runs across Lexington Avenue.

"Yo, I *tawht youz* wasn't *comin'*," Sal says, locking me in a big junkie bear hug full of relief that the source of dope and/or dope money has arrived. "Papi *wuz wonderin'* where *youz* at too."

"Traffic sucks," I say. "It's the Friday after Thanksgiving."

"My *mutha wuz* bummed out *youz* couldn't make it *fawh dinnah yestuhday*," Sal says. "She wanted to meet *youz*, Bobby."

Sal invited me to Thanksgiving dinner with his mother in Bay Ridge, Brooklyn, but I declined. Now, in retrospect, given the wretched disaster of my own Thanksgiving, it might have been a good idea.

"Maybe another time," I say. "It was nice of your mother to invite me."

"She appreciates what *youz* do *fawh* me," he says.

Sal's mother thinks he works for me. Ours is a telephone relationship—when I call, she cries and tells me what a hopeless slime Sal is. I listen, make sympathetic sounds and offer words of support and encouragement.

"Maybe *youz* can come *fawh* Christmas," Sal says.

"I'm supposed to be with my family," I say.

"*Youz* is *comin'* up *fawh* Christmas to be *wit yawh* family in Jersey?"

"Yeah, my girlfriend's supposed to come too."

"Yo, *dat* would be great, Bobby. I *wanna* meet her."

That would work well. She *threw a drumstick at me* for not helping with Thanksgiving dinner. She'll *shoot me* if she finds out I'm shooting dope and hanging out with guys like Sal in Harlem.

"We broke up last night," I say.

"What happened?" Sal says. "I *tawht youz* guys was tight."

"She's pissed that I didn't help with dinner."

"*Dat's* bad, Bobby. *Youz* know *dey* like *youz tah* help *wit dinnah*. She's gonna be pissed *fawh* a while."

"Is Papi around?"

"Yeah. He went inside the *stawh fawh* a minute. *Youz* still want five bundles?"

"I want six. What brand does he have?"

"Murder One," Sal says.

"Is the Murder One still good?"

"I wouldn't let *youz* buy it if it wasn't no *muthafuckin'* good."

The girl who was standing across Lexington Avenue with Sal is watching us.

"Who's your friend?" I say.

"She's a *custahmah*," Sal says. "She's a *bankah* from *Westchestah*."

A banker?

"What's she, a teller?" I say.

"She ain't no *telluh*, Bobby," Sal says. "She's, like, a *kawhpawhrate* loan *offisuh*."

"You're kidding."

"I ain't *kiddin' youz*. She works *fawh* one *ah dem* big banks. Chase Manhattan *awh sumtin'*. She comes on the weekends."

"No shit."

"Really. She *skawhs* a bundle *awh two fawh* the week every Satuhday. *Youz wanna* meet her? If *youz* like her, maybe *youz* could fuck her *befawh youz* go back to D.C. *Youz* got *rubbahs*? I got *sum* if *youz* need *'em*."

Sal shouts, "Yo, Karen! Yo, Karen, *com'ere*!"

She crosses Lexington Avenue.

"Karen," Sal says. "*Dis* is Bobby. He's like my *brutha*."

I nod and say, "Nice to meet you," like we're standing in line at a deli being introduced by a mutual friend.

"Bobby," Sal says. "*Dis* is Karen. She's good people."

Karen shakes my hand and says, "Nice to meet you."

I look across the street and see our Dominican dealer standing at his payphone.

"There's Papi," I say.

"*Youz* want me *tah* get the stuff, Bobby?" Sal says.

I hand Sal six hundred dollars in fifties.

Karen stares at it.

"*Youz* want me *tah* get *yawhz* too, Karen?" Sal says.

"Sure," she says, also handing him money. "A bundle."

"I'll be back *inna* few minutes," Sal says. "Just hang out. I *gotta* go *wit* Papi *tah* get the bundles. He *ain't holdin' dat* much shit. But be careful. TNT's around."

Great. TNT is the Tactical Narcotics Taskforce, plainclothes cops who ride around in unmarked cars and taxis and do jump outs. As in, jumping out of cars and arresting you.

No crime in standing on a Harlem street corner with a chick.

Sal walks back across Lexington Avenue. He says something to our dealer. The Dominican nods. They walk north on Lexington Avenue.

"You come up here a lot?" Karen says.

"Every now and then," I say. "I'm from D.C."

"You're from Washington? You come all the way up here for dope?"

"Every couple of weeks. Or a friend of mine comes up."

"I come on the weekend and get enough for the week."

"You work for a bank?" I say. "What do you do?"

"I'm a loan officer in Westchester."

"Cool," I say. "I'm a reporter."

"Really?"

Sal returns with the drugs as we chat about dope, Harlem and work. There is no way to detach from him and go off with the female banker junkie, so we grab a livery cab and head back downtown. Many, many dozens of blocks worth of slow traffic later, we arrive at the Hotel Pennsylvania, a massive lodging on Seventh Avenue that's anonymous and right across the street from Penn Station.

"I *ain't nevuh* been *tah* the Hotel *Pee-Yay befawh*," Sal says as we enter the huge and busy lobby.

It may, in fact, be the only hotel to which Sal has ever been that doesn't rent rooms by the hour.

"We'll be fine here for the afternoon," I say.

"It looks like it *kawhsts* a lot," he says.

"I've got it covered."

"We could go to *dat* place on 27th where we went last time."

The place on 27th Street Sal is referring to is a "short stay" hotel (with "stays" being as short as it takes one to get off either via drugs or exchange of bodily fluids) infested with crack whores in which we've smoked crack and shot dope.

"Don't this place *kawhst* a lot?" Sal says. "We could probably buy *anutha* bundle with what we're gonna spend."

"Keep your voice down," I say.

"*Sawhry*. But, what's this place *kawhst*? A buck fifty? That's *anutha* ten, fifteen bags *ah* dope *awh* a shitload *ah* rock."

"Lower…your…voice. We're in the middle of a hotel lobby."

"I'm *sawhry*. I ain't loud am I, Karen?"

"Yeah, you are," she says.

"*Awhls* I'm *sayin'* is why spend money here when youz can spend it on dope *an'* rock?" Sal says.

"Lower your voice!" I growl. "The whole goddamned hotel can hear you."

"*Awhright. Awhright. Jeez,* Bobby, *sumtin' botherin' youz?*"

"Don't worry," I say. "This will be my treat. It's the holidays. Merry Christmas. You guys wait here while I get a room."

I approach the desk and get the room without any problem. I pay cash.

Sal and Karen are waiting for me. I hold up the card that opens the door. The room is on the tenth floor.

The elevator up is packed. Sal, Karen and I crowd into a corner. When Sal starts to say something, I cut him off and ask him to wait until we get upstairs—the last thing I want is a discourse about dope in the elevator.

The room is on the Seventh Avenue side of the hotel, overlooking the Garden.

"Yo, Bobby, *dis* is nice," Sal says, flopping into a chair near the window.

Karen takes off her coat and sits on the bed.

"I'm glad we have someplace decent to hang out for a while," she says. "This is great."

I take my coat off and sit on the bed near her.

Sal gets up and turns on the TV. He puts on *All My Children* and retreats to his chair holding the remote.

"Do you have to put that on?" I say.

"I love *Awhl My Children,*" he says. "I *nevah* get to see it *cuz* I'm out in the *aftahnoon.*"

I take out a bundle, my teaspoon and a syringe, and fix myself a shot of dope. Karen snorts a bag. I go into the bathroom and shoot up, happy that I find a vein without turning myself into a pincushion.

I'm buzzed when I exit the bathroom. Sal looks at me hungrily. No words needed. I hand him a bag and he asks me for a syringe.

I know what's coming. Watching Sal shoot dope is a horror. After years of injecting heroin, he can hardly find a vein.

He sits back down in the chair by the window. Ten minutes later, he's standing in front of me saying, "Fuck. *Cocksucka.* Shit. *Muthafucka.*"

"Maybe if I go into the *crappah,*" he says. "*Youz* guys is making me nervous."

He goes into the bathroom.

He is still cursing. Things are slamming.

Karen sighs and says that it would be great if we could get rid of him and hang out alone.

The cursing and thrashing noises stop. I knock on the bathroom door.

Sal says, "Yo."

I go inside.

Dear God.

There is blood all over the floor. The hotel towels are stained with blood that he's been wiping up.

It looks so bad, I'm afraid he's going to die from blood loss.

"Hey, Bobby," Sal says. "I got the shot off."

I shake my head and say, "It looks like somebody got murdered in here."

"It *ain't nuttin'*," Sal says. "I'll clean it up. *Gimme* a minute *tah* get *awhf.*"

"What the fuck happened?"

"I had a hard time."

"Christ."

"I got it. Don't worry. I'll clean it."

"We're going to have to get rid of the towels or the maids will call the cops."

"Fuck 'em. They ain't seen blood *befawh*?"

I have an idea.

"After you clean up, you want to go back up to 123rd for rock?" I say.

"Rock" is the magic word. Sal's eyes light up.

"*Youz* guys *wanna* go all the way back there?" he says.

"If I give you fifty bucks and subway fare, will you go?" I say.

I know that giving Sal money and expecting him to come back with crack is an exercise in futility. The only things he will come back with are excuses for not coming back with drugs:

He was mugged.

He got beat.

He ran into somebody he owed money who was going to kill him unless he paid up.

A very aggressive New York City pigeon pecked his pocket and flew off with the money.

Etc.

Fuck it. Karen has suggested getting rid of our Third Wheel. Giving Sal money for drugs is the best and fastest way to lose him.

"Yeah, sure," Sal says, taking the bait. "Maybe Karen'll come *wit* me."

"No," I say. "I think she wants to hang here."

"Okay. *Whatevah*."

I hand Sal sixty dollars.

Five minutes later, Sal is on his way out the door, leaving us to enjoy the Hotel *Pee-Yay* in peace for the rest of the afternoon.

Manhattan Masala

It is getting dark in Manhattan and the rush hour traffic is building.

The cab that Sal and I are taking back uptown from Chinatown is mired in congealed traffic on Park Avenue in the East Sixties.

"*Youz wanna' geddout* and walk, Bobby?" Sal says.

"All the way to 125th Street?" I say.

"I mean *fawh* a little ways. We can walk to the train and take dat."

"What's the rush?"

Sal's in a hurry? His main responsibilities in life are getting methadone every day from a clinic in Harlem and selling it to buy drugs. Granted, the daily hustle to get dope money and cop drugs is nerve-racking, but Sal's life can't be *that* complicated. I've got to sustain a sizeable dope habit while keeping enough of a grip to maintain the professional reporting career that allows the monstrous Jones to flourish in the first place.

I need to run back to Washington so I can write a five-page magazine story that's due in less than twenty-four hours. I haven't written a sentence of it yet.

The faster I can finish buying drugs in New York and get on a Metroliner at Penn Station, the better.

"Nah, Bobby, I ain't stressed," Sal says. "But my *mutha* wants me home in time *fawh* dinner cuz I'm *bringin'* food *fawh* dinner."

Mother Sal trusts him to put food on the table?

Isn't she afraid of starving to death?

Sal would trade the groceries for a two-dollar vial of rock.

Or, a three-dollar vial.

At best.

"Relax," I say. "If it gets late, you can call your mother so she won't worry."

"She *ain't worryin',*" he says. "She just *wantsa* know about dinner. I told my *mutha youz* was *payin'* me today *fawh* the work I been *doin' fawh youz*, so I'm *treatin'* tonight."

In a different context Sal's devotion would be heartwarming, but in this one, it's lacking a certain something.

We are at East 71st Street and Park Avenue. The heart of Very Expensive New York.

Sal takes a vial of Green Top crack from his pocket and a glass stem you smoke it with from his pocket and says, "*Yo*, Bobby, *youz* don't mind if I do a hit, do *youz*?"

In the backseat of a cab on Park Avenue?

With old ladies in furs walking bizarrely coiffed miniature French Poodles and irritatingly perky Jack Russell Terriers on the sidewalk?

Has he lost his mind?

"Fuck no," I say.

"Good, Bobby, *cuz* it'll make me feel *bettah*," Sal says.

He opens a vial of crack and pours the off-white rocks into the stem.

"I mean, fuck yes, I mind," I say. "Are you nuts?"

"*Wha*'?" Sal says.

"Sal!"

Fortunately, the cabbie is oblivious. Indian music is blaring from the radio and he's concentrating on squeezing between barely moving cars in a cab driverly way. "Put it away!" I say. "Not now!"

"Just one little hit," he says.

For starters, there is no such thing as *one little hit*, when it comes to crack.

This is one of the major issues associated with doing the drug.

Sal becomes a crack-obsessed moron the moment he starts smoking.

"No!" I say.

It is to no avail.

Sal ducks. He leans toward the door. He lights the cocaine in the stem. The crack sizzles.

He sits up, holding his breath, rolls down the window and blows a large cloud of crack smoke out the window onto Park Avenue.

The cabbie looks in the rear view.

Dyspeptic Indian music is still blaring from the radio.

We're on the Upper East Side of Manhattan, but it's like being in a mobile crackhouse in Dehli.

"No *zmoking, blease,*" the driver says, like Sal just lit up a Marlboro.

"Sorry," I say. "He won't do it again. No smoking, Sal."

"*Tank youz*, Bobby," Sal says. "*Fuckin'* A. *Dat's* good shit. *Youz wanna'* try some?"

Sal is still holding the crack stem in plain view, so I say, "No! Put it away, Sal."

"*Youz* got it, Bobby," he says. "I'm just *waitin' fawh* it to cool off. If I put it away now, I'll get burnt."

At this particular point in time, I don't care if he goes up in flames.

Smoking crack in a cab is not on the list of things I want to do today.

Hyperactive sitar twangs and percussion sounds continue emanating from the front of the cab. The driver, thankfully, is totally fixated on getting through traffic.

I shake my head. Sal, who is now amped up from smoking the rock, is babbling about setting up a business to transport dope from New York to D.C.

"*Tink* about it, Bobby" he says. "*Wit yawh* connections, *youz* could hook us up good. Neither one of us would *evah havetah* worry about *buyin'* dope again and I could visit *youz*."

Oh yeah. This is *exactly* what I'd like to introduce the neighbors to. Maybe we could turn my place into a crackhouse and shooting gallery while we're at it. It would give the people on the condo board something to talk about besides whether or not people can leave doormats in the hall in front of their doors.

"I don't think so, Sal," I say.

"*Youz* don't want me to come to D.C.?" he says. He has a crestfallen look on his face again that indicates the potential onset of horrible junkie tears.

How can I explain that he won't blend?

"I don't want to get involved in bringing a lot of drugs from New York to D.C.," I say.

Strictly speaking, this is very much the truth.

"*Ain't dat* what *youz* is *doin' awhlready*?" he says.

"It's only for me and a friend," I say. "It's different."

"Well, maybe, I could come *anyways*? I'd bring shit only *fawh youz* and I could come, right?"

"Sure, Sal. Soon. Okay?"

"Really?"

"Sure."

"*Fuckin'A. Youz* could take me to the White House."

Absolutely. That would be my hope. I'm certain we'd be received warmly.

"And to the Congress," he adds.

"We'll see," I say.

"Good. In a *coupla'* weeks. *Youz* can send me the money *fawh* the dope and if *youz* pay me *aheadah* time, I can use the money *fawh* the train. *Dat* way I *don't gotta' botha* my *mutha fawh* it."

Sounds like a plan.

Sal looks like he's going to put the crack stem away, but instead, he reaches into his pocket and extracts another vial of the crack he bought in Chinatown.

He pours the crack into the stem and says, "Don't worry, Bobby, it'll only take a second."

"No!" I say.

But Sal is already ducking and lighting the stem.

The drugs are sizzling.

He sits back, holding his breath.

Then, he rolls down the window and blows another cloud of crack smoke into traffic.

"No *zmoking* in cab, *blease*!" the driver shouts over the Indian music blasting from the radio. "*Blease*! Or *ve* stop and you go."

An Eastern wail is *wahahahahahahahahing* on the radio over the sitars, sarods, harmoniums, tamburas, tablahs and other percussion instruments.

This is becoming surreal.

To the driver, I say, "I'm sorry. I'm really sorry. It won't happen again."

To Sal, I say, "Put the fucking stem away. Wait until we get to Harlem and you can smoke it all. I don't care."

"It's a *fuckin'* shame," Sal says.

"Huh?"

"Don't nobody *drivin'* no cabs speak English no mawh."

"Who cares? Put the stem away, Sal."

"Hey, no problem, Bobby. I couldn't help it. I *wuz losin'* my buzz."

Finally, the cab hits the lower reaches of Harlem and breaks free of the traffic. In a matter of minutes, we're back at 123rd and Lexington Avenue, where we started hours ago before heading downtown on a ridiculous, and unsuccessful quest, for Chinese Rock.

I pay the driver and throw in a huge tip, if not for his trouble, then for not calling the cops.

We get out.

Sal surveys the streetscape. Our drug dealer is gone.

"*Muthafucka*'," he says. "Popi *ain't* here."

"That's okay," I say. "I should get going. I have to get home."

"*Youz don't* want *nuttin'* else? There's *uddah* dope around. We can go to the Sout Bronx."

"The South Bronx?"

"It's right *ovah* the bridge. Alls we *gotta'* do is walk. I know where to get good shit in the *Sout* Bronx."

"I don't want to go to the South Bronx."

"I go *dere awhl* the time," he says. "I'm *witcha. Ain't nuttin' gonna'* happen. We'll cop and go. It'll take a half *howah.*"

"I don't want to go to the South Bronx."

"Dey got good shit in the Sout Bronx, Bobby."

"No," I say. "Either we find something around here or I'm leaving."

"*Yo,* don't get mad. I'm just *tryin'* to get *youz* the best shit. We'll find *sumtin'* on First Avenue."

"Let's go."

Sal and I walk to First Avenue and 123rd.

"*Whaddahyouz* want?" he says.

I tell him to get two more bundles—at ten dime bags per bundle—and give him two hundred dollars.

"Wait here," he says.

I watch Sal walk up the block and disappear around the corner. Five minutes later, he's coming back down the block toward me.

"You get it?" I say.

"Yeah," he says. "The guy says it's good, but he wouldn't *lemme* taste any and *youz* don't *wanna'* go to the *Sout* Bronx, so don't blame me if *youz* don't like it."

"I'm sure it'll be fine."

"*Youz* want *anyting* else?"

"No. I should go."

It's six. With traffic, I'll be lucky if I make a seven o'clock train.

"Why don't we go *sumplace fawh* a minute so *youz* can get off *befawh youz* go?" Sal says.

"Yeah," I say. "But let's make it fast."

We walk to an empty lot between two abandoned buildings a couple of blocks away. An old truck—like one that delivers bread or potato chips, only covered with graffiti—is in the middle of the lot. We duck behind it.

I open a bag of the new dope and quickly sniff it.

Not bad.

Sal, meanwhile, puts two vials of crack in the stem and lights up.

"Why don't I take my stuff?" I say when he finishes exhaling smoke.

"No problem, Bobby," he says.

Sal hands me 38 bags of dope, one Thai stick, nine Valium, six Ativan and six vials of crack. I give him the Ativan and the crack and tell him to keep them. Then I give him fifty dollars, which is his "pay."

"*Tanks*, Bobby," he says. "*Youz* is good to me."

I put the drugs in various nooks and crannies of my coat.

We walk back to Lexington Avenue.

I flag down a livery cab and tell Sal I'll see him soon.

"*Tanks*, Bobby," he says. "*Kawhl* me tonight."

"Huh?" I say.

"*Kawhl* me when *youz* get home. I *wanna'* make sure *youz* get *dere* okay. *Uddahwise* I'm gonna' worry."

Like I'm going to get mugged in the toilet on the Metroliner?

"Okay," I say. "I'll call."

Sal trudges away. I get in the cab and tell the driver to take me to Penn Station.

He looks at me over his shoulder and groans. We take off down Lexington Avenue.

On the day after Christmas

On the day after Christmas, the streets of Harlem are buzzing with holiday cheer and the nervous energy of junkies trying to hustle the shit that Santa left and turn it into money that will procure the only gifts that ever, ever count:

Heroin.

Crack.

Coke.

Methadone.

Valium.

Ativan.

Xanax.

Percoset.

Hennessy.

And, for those that simply want some herbal cheer in their post-Christmas revelry, some good, old-fashioned New York City dime bags of street weed, the smoke so nice you don't even have to hit it twice. Unless you want to.

I must contend with the exchange-and-return-thing tomorrow, having a gift certificate whose stated use is for purchasing sneakers. Turning the gift certificate into cash with which I can procure dope is a desirable use of the gift, even if it is a perversion of both the spirit in which it was given and the purpose for which it is intended.

I received the gift certificate because a close relative wanted to ensure that I buy a legitimate gift rather than drugs.

It is a creepy attempt at behavior modification.

I am a consenting adult.

A man with a brain.

I will do what I want. When I want. And, how I want.

Fifty dollars is fifty dollars, and those fifty bucks will be used to buy five-dime bags of Fuji Power or DOA or whatever brand is happening so that I can get a good dope buzz on. Tomorrow will be devoted to browbeating a store manager into giving me a cash refund on the gift certificate. If he or she refuses, citing unbending store policy, I will stomp and scream and shout about corporate robbery until (a). I get my way because the scene I am creating is bad for business or

(b). Get escorted from the store by security.

I can always *steal* some sneakers or shoes when I need them, whereas dope is something I have to buy.

In the meantime, I have $250 in real dollars in my pocket, courtesy of cash Christmas gifts—the best present under the sun—and some shoplifted DVDs returned for cash refunds to a retail chain at which I worked before being fired for contributing to the store's shrinkage rate and whose weaknesses I know intimately and can exploit with ease.

I am in the money, at least, by junkie standards.

(*Important note to junkies who are not yet so smacked out they can not hold down a job*: If you must work a low-paying job to feed your monkey, work retail and angle for a job at the register. While it's impossible to support a respectable dope habit on minimum wage, it is quite possible to keep up a treading-water dope habit on minimum wage + the spoils of insider theft. An added benefit of supplementing slave wages with petty theft is that it allows you to wage a personal war of subversion against bloodsucking corporate capitalism. This, in turn, enables you to consider yourself a social activist and agent of change instead of being, well, just a junkie. Be sure only to work for and steal from especially odious human- and worker-rights abusing chains, big box retailers and multinationals to help you support your dope habit. Fuck Wal-Mart, not the little guy.)

Personally speaking, it has not been a bad Christmas. I did not have high overhead because I went *Christmas shoplifting* rather than *Christmas shopping*. All from the same store at the same suburban New Jersey shopping center. Walking right out the front door a *half-dozen* times with shopping bags stuffed full of shoplifted books, DVDs and CDs. I stripped the merchandise of security strips, alarm tags and other devices as I was comfortably seated in one of the chairs the retailer provides around the store, and I did not worry about store security, which I knew for a fact the retailer does not have, or the employees, who I also know for a fact wouldn't care if you walked out pulling a trailer full of boosted goods.

Needless to say, I gave a lot of books, CDs and DVDs.

This may or may not say something about the point in life to which narcotics have delivered me, a formerly respectable reporter, but such underhandedness allows me to get on with the obligations of life and keeps me in dope, and that's all that matters.

I ponder these things, as the taxi in which I'm riding gets closer to my destination. We are on the upper, ass end of Park Avenue, a stretch of real estate that bears only the most distant of relationships with its Upper East Side cousin—i.e. they both exist on the same planet in the same country in the same city.

We drive past knots of people passing around merchandise.

In one sweep of my eyes around a windswept and chilly intersection beneath the elevated Metro North train tracks through which swirls an astounding amount of trash, one sees all of the abundance of the American consumer market on display:

Hats.

Shirts.

Gloves.

CDs.

CD players.

Electric shavers.

Blow dryers.

Etc.

It is like a Bad Karma Flea Market from Hell, a forlorn place in which the fruits of Christmas giving are turned into potential vehicles for a free high.

Most places in America, holiday returns are part of a timeworn ritual in which the recipient trades in the unwanted gift (atrocious tie, two sizes too small shirt, CD already in the collection), receives a store credit and, in turn, purchases something he or she *really* wants.

And so,

The Ugly Tie from Aunt Jessica = The Cool Shirt You Really Wanted.

Or,

The Boring Book about the Reagan Administration from Your Mother + The Huge Coffee Table Art Book of Monet Paintings from Your Big Sister = The Joy Division Box CD Set You've Been Meaning to Get.

Not in the Land of Refined Opiate Product Sold in Ten-Dollar Bags.

Nooooo.

Here, the cash return—or, at least, the dream that it can be so—rules.

It is a great day to get a bargain if you are not a junkie or if you are a junkie with cash that can be spent on something other than dope.

I tell the driver to pull over, walk a couple of blocks and quickly find Sal.

"Yo, Bobby," he says. "Merry Christmas! Fuckin' A!"

Instantly, by the volume of his voice, I can tell that Sal is loaded. Generally, Sal is only truly wasted on the First of the Month, when the Social Security disability check he receives for being a junkie arrives, or when I purchase dope for him.

"Hey, Sal," I say. "Merry Christmas."

"Merry Christmas, Bobby!" Sal says, wiping crud from around his mouth with the sleeve of the battered brown leather jacket that he wears winter, spring, summer and fall. "My *mutha wuz askin' fawh youz yestahday*. She *wuz hopin' youz wuz comin' ovah fawh some canoli awh sfolgliatelle*."

Of all the junkies in New York, I've got to find an Italian one from Brooklyn with a mother that invites me over for holiday pastry.

"I told you I couldn't come for Christmas," I say.

"I know. But she really *wantsa* meet *youz*, Bobby. *Yawh*, like, special to her."

"We've only talked on the phone, Sal."

"But she appreciates what *youz* do *fawh* me. I *tawhk* about *youz awhl* the time."

"I know, Sal."

Sal's mutha believes that he works for me and that I am paying him to be my research assistant. She is on the right track, but very much on the wrong train. I am paying Sal a modest amount, in either cash or dope, to purchase dope for me so that I don't get ripped off or busted on the streets of Harlem.

"I got a Christmas treat *fawh youz*, Bobby," Sal says.

"What's that?"

"I *awhlready* got us *sum* rock. We don't *gotta* worry about *coppin'* right now. Shit's crazy anyways. Too many people walkin' around wit too much money *tahday*. Some *ah* the *muthafuckin'* dope spots got lines right now."

New York City is the only place in all of America where junkies line up for dope the same way people line up to buy mega million dollar jackpot lottery tickets. And no one, first and foremost the police, pay the dope lines any mind. As though, 100 junkies standing in line in the dead of winter in Harlem are lined up for a Bill Clinton book signing.

I look at Sal incredulously and say, "You bought some rock for us?"

If Sal has money to get drugs without getting money from me first, Santa Claus really must have come knocking yesterday.

"Don't look so *fuckin'* surprised," Sal says. "*Yawh hurtin'* my feelings."

"Sorry. You have rock?"

"I had some Christmas presents. My *mutha* gave me shit like *sweatahs* and shirts and she'll get upset if I sell *'em.* But I told *youz* about my Uncle Richie, my *fatha's brutha* who went to jail *wit* him?"

"Yeah."

"Uncle Richie gave me a hundred bucks *fawh* Christmas and told me *tah* use it *tah* buy myself *sumtin'* nice. So, I got *fahwty* deuces in my pocket."

Sal's got 40 $2 vials of crack? Dude.

"You want to go someplace to smoke?" I say. "I mean, I'll pay you back with more rock later. I could use a blast."

"Sure, Bobby," he says. "Kyeisha, this chick on 122nd Street, is home. She gotta place. It's cool as *lawhng* as you don't let her *dawtuh* hit *youz* up *fawh* no rock."

We walk four blocks to a somewhat scabrous block of 122nd Street. Sal stops in front of a four-story apartment buildings and screams, "Kyeisha, yo! Yo, Kyeisha! Yo! It's Sal! Yo! Open *dah* window! Yo, Kyeisha!"

A window opens and a twentysomething black female pokes her head out the window.

"Yo, you *bettah* stop *screamin*' like *dat*," she says.

"*Sawhry*," Sal shouts. "I got my friend Bobby *wit* me. Can we chill *wit youz*?"

The head disappears. A minute later, she is standing at the front door. We follow her up four flights of stairs redolent of piss and greasy fried food into her apartment.

Sade is on the CD player. There is a Christmas tree near the window. The apartment smells of crack cocaine and fried chicken.

"Bobby's a *writah,*" Sal says by way of introduction.

I sit down on a battered chair.

"Oh yeah?" Kyeisha says. "You *wanna'* write a book '*bout* me?"

"Where's T-Bone?" Sal says, and tells me that T-Bone, so-called, is Kyseisha's male partner.

"He out on the street tryin' to sell Christmas shit and hustle up sum cash, but now that you and you friend here, Sal, we be *chillin' anyways*, right?"

An 18-or-so-year-old female comes from another room. She looks me up and down and nods at Sal.

"Who you friend be, Sal?" she says.

"*Dat's* Bobby," he says. "He's a *writuh.*"

"Oh, yeah, you *gonna'* write '*bout* us?" she says.

"Fuck no," Sal says. "We're here *tah* do *sum* blasts."

"Now you *tawhkin'*," the younger female, whose name is Crystal, says. "You wanna' sell me *sum* blasts for this Tupac CD I got yesterday? I don't know why people *givin'* me Tupac. I don't like no Tupac."

And, so it goes, on the day after the holiday that came before.

Relatively Beat

I am driving in a large circle through summertime Harlem, from 143rd and Lenox Avenue, down to 125th and Lexington, and back again—with smaller intersecting circles around various blocks in the vicinity of 125th and Lex—looking for Gavi and Madeleine, my Puerto Rican dope connections.

I am on the third such large go-round and umpteenth small roundabout of the afternoon, and I still can't find them. Strange. Junkies are creatures of *extreme* habit. They don't stray far from home or the street corners on which they usually hang because changes in routine interfere with life's most important activities: copping dope and getting off.

They are nowhere to be found either on their home block, which is 143rd Street immediately west of Lenox Avenue, or in their copping area, which is within a quarter-mile radius of 125th and Lex. Currently, I'm driving on East 127th Street, having just gotten off the southbound Harlem River Drive.

I've got a hundred dollars in my pocket courtesy of CDs stolen from my workplace and resold at a used CD shop and a Jones that's already asserting itself in sneezes and sniffles.

The clock is ticking.

I park my '81 sky blue BMW on 129th near Lexington, thinking that I might find Gavi and/or Madeleine if I'm on foot. If not, I'll hit one of the dope spots myself.

Relying on others to cop for me is wimpy, but safe. On my own, I am at risk of:

(A). Getting ripped off while buying dope.

(B). Being sold dummy bags full of crap rather than dope.

(C). Getting ripped off after buying dope, or

(D). Not getting ripped off at all because:

(1). I get stopped by the cops on the way to cop.
(2). I get busted while buying dope, or
(3). I get busted after buying dope.

I'm likely to score and walk away with my dope un-robbed and un-busted, but my fears aren't entirely irrational. I can only be one of several things on some of the East Harlem blocks I frequent:
(A). Slightly insane.
(B). A social worker.
(C). A real estate speculator trying to get way out in front of the wave.
(D). A cop, or
(E). A junkie.

Over the years on the streets of Harlem, I have been called things like *Poh*-leece, Cracker, White Boy, *Poh*-leece *muthafucker*, Cracker *muthafucker* and, occasionally, Baby, or Papi by Latina crackwhores and Latino crack dealers.

I can deal with the names, but my real fear is the real police.

The cops, specifically the Tactical Narcotics Taskforce or TNT, periodically do "jump outs." While word spreads fast on Jump Out Days, jump outs can happen at any point.

TNT favors yellow and livery cabs, making East Harlem one of the few places in New York City where a taxi on the wrong street can put the fear of God into you for reasons that have nothing to do with road rage.

All in all, I prefer having Gavi and Madeleine do my dirty work for me, just like Sal, my dope buddy from Brooklyn, did my bidding in Harlem before I had to lose him because he'd become a thieving and insane pain in the ass.

As soon as I turn south on Lexington, the sales pitches from the junkies peddling methadone and pills start coming fast and furious.

"Got twenty," a Latino guy with a wild beard and matted black hair says, veering into my path. "Twenty. Sealed. Twenty."

"Twenty" is the quantity of methadone he's selling, as in 20 milligrams. "Sealed," meanwhile, alleges that the bottle of meth hasn't been opened, as opposed to being "spit back," which is what they call methadone that the junkie has put in his mouth while being watched by methadone clinic staff and, then, *spit back* into the bottle from whence it came and offered for sale.

Spit Back is an especially vile and desperate way to do drugs, in that:

(A). It is methadone, one of the more atrocious drugs known to mankind and a product of World War II Nazi pharmaceutical R&D.

And…

(B). There is no high in the world worth swallowing a cocktail of methadone and slimy junkie saliva.

"Ativan," an older black guy in filthy khakis mutters a few steps further down the block. "Ativan. Valium. Xanax. Ativan."

"*Tirty*," says another Latino guy with no front teeth. "*Tirty*. Got *tirty*."

"Got Valium," a younger Latino in his twenties offers. "Many as *chu wan*."

It's an open-air supermarket for drugs you don't want when you're on the market for dope.

I push through the knots of junkies and meth and pill dealers, trying not to inhale too much of the summertime street funk of unwashed bodies and festering garbage, and stand on the corner of 125th and Lex peering at the mass of people.

Gavi and Madeleine are not on the northeast corner. Likewise the southeast, southwest and northwest corners.

I look east down 125th Street where Gavi sometimes hangs out to sell the (sealed) bottles of methadone he is given at the clinic he frequents. Like most New York junkies, Gavi doesn't take his methadone. He sells his publicly-provided free methadone and uses the proceeds to buy privately-provided $10 bags of dope.

It is what happens when government programs and the free market intersect.

I look across Lexington Avenue at the fast food place that sells fried chicken, *platanos*, empanadas and other Latino food where Gavi and Madeleine sometimes hang out.

They're not there either.

Fuck.

I walk past the vacant lot on the southeast corner of 125th and Lexington Avenue that's slated to become a shopping center and will cause a huge upheaval in the drug marketplace by uplifting the quality of life so much that the dealers and junkies have to find other corners on which to hang.

I continue south on Lex toward 123rd Street and the bodega where the old Latino guy I used to cop dope from with Sal hung out. He's been gone for a couple of years and the only things currently sold on that corner are bebidas and cervezas.

I'm so happy when I see Gavi and Madeline standing across Lexington on 124th Street that I almost cry.

"Gavi!" I yell. "Madi!"

Seeing me, they wave and cross the street.

"*Chu jus'* get here?" Gavi says, shaking my hand.

"I've been looking for you for a couple of hours."

"We *dun* go *nowheres*," Madeleine says.

"We *dun* see you," Gavi says.

"I drove here and back up to the apartment twice," I say. "This is my third time."

"I *tol chu* was Bob, Gavi!" Madeleine says.

"She *screamin'* at *chu* car like she crazy," Gavi says. "But *chu dun* see us."

"*Chu* was *drivin'* too *fas'*," Madeleine says.

"Fuck. I've been driving in circles forever. What's around?"

"*Ain'* shit," Gavi says. "Place hot."

"Gavi *almos'* get busted by TNT," Madeleine says.

"What happened?" I say.

"They do a jump out on 120th," Gavi says. "They stop me."

"*Tanks* God he *wun holdin'*," Madeleine says.

"They pop me," Gavi says. "I'm fucked. *Chu* know I got parole."

"I know."

"They *chould* lock up criminals, not people *doin'* dope," Madeleine says.

"Fuckin' *marecon* cops," Gavi adds.

"When was the jump out?" I ask.

"This *mornin' roun'* eleven," Gavi says.

I look at my watch. It's nearly five.

"You think it's cooled off?" I say.

"I *dunno*," Gavi says. "*Thins* quiet."

"Where the car?" Madeleine says. "*Chu chouldn'* be *walkin' roun'*."

"It's on 129th," I say.

We walk back to 129th Street and get in the car. Gavi wants to try an apartment building on First Avenue where dope and rock are usually on sale.

I give him 80 dollars and drop him off on the corner. I circle the block with Madeleine.

"I hope *nuthin'* happen," Madeleine says, looking nervously in the side view mirror.

"I'm sure it'll be okay," I say, totally unsure that anything is going to be okay and nervously checking my rear view mirror to see if any yellow cabs are following me.

We circle the block a half dozen times while waiting for Gavi to reappear. Finally, we spot him on the corner of 122nd Street and First Avenue.

I pull over. He climbs into the back seat.

"Everything okay?" I say.

"I *thin* so," Gavi says. "I *bough'* the dope from a black guy. I *dun* like *buyin'* from black guys."

Gavi is not a big believer in racial tolerance or diversity.

"What brand is it?" I say.

New York City heroin bears brand names stamped in ink on the bags:

Fuji Power.

D.O.A.

Midnight.

Murder One.

Etc.

"Killer," he says. "I wanted to try it, but he *wouldn'* let me. The *marecon* say the block too hot. Ain't no other shit *roun'*."

Killer is not a familiar brand.

"I'm sure it'll be okay," I say, hopefully.

We drive off. Gavi tears open a bag and snorts about half the contents.

A minute later, he says, "Shit. I *dunno,* man."

"What's wrong?" I say.

"I *thin* is dummy bags," he says.

The dummy bag filled with God knows what is the junkie's worst nightmare.

"You sure?"

"Yeah, I thin so. Fuck!"

"Fuck!"

"I'm gonna go back."

"*Wha' chu* crazy *papi*?" Madeleine says.

"I *ain't gettin'* beat," he says. "*Less* go back."

"How many did you get?" I say.

"*Tanks* God I *chus* get four," Gavi says. "I *din* trust the *muthafucker*."

"Then, why you buy it?" Madeleine says.

"Cause ain't *nuthin* else *aroun'*," Gavi says.

"You *chouldn'* do that," she says.

They argue in Spanish.

"You still have forty bucks?" I interrupt.

"Yeah," Gavi says.

"Let's find something else."

"No. I *gonna fine* that *marecon*. Maybe I *fine* the manager."

Dope, like any business, has its own hierarchy. On the street retail end, there are salesmen who sell the bags. There are runners who get the product from the main stash, which never stays with the salesman. And there are managers, who oversee the entire enterprise.

"Let's just go," I say.

"No," Gavi says. "I *gonna fine* this *marecon*."

We drive back to the dope spot.

Gavi gets out of the car. Ten minutes later, he's back again.

"The *marecon* who sole me the dummy bags *wun* there," he says. "But I fine the manager."

"And?" I say.

"I *tole* him what happen, but he *wun* do *nuthin'*. At *lease*, he got dope. I try before I buy."

"You got some?" I say, relieved that we've got dope rather than pissed about the rip off.

Relatively beat is better than totally beat.

"Yeah," Gavi says. "I figure you *wan* me to."

"Yeah."

A yellow cab cruises past and continues on First Avenue. I pull out into traffic, in a hurry to get out of the neighborhood before something else goes wrong.

Dog Days

I am sitting in my 1981 sky blue BMW on West 142nd Street and Lenox Avenue in front of a boarded up tenement in Harlem. It is a stiflingly hot August evening.

Across the Harlem River, the hazy sky above the Bronx is glowing white from the lights at Yankee Stadium. Glumly, I watch Puerto Rican and Dominican kids from the neighborhood playing in the gushing water from an open fire hydrant on the corner.

When the occasional anemic breeze blows in from the river, I catch a nauseating whiff of the rotting Harlem trash that's been marinating in the blazing August sun all day long. It's garbage day, but nothing's been picked up yet, so the overwhelming neighborhood aroma is *Basura Con Pollo Frito.*

I sneeze, which is an indication of imminent dope sickness. Then, with the next breath of noxious garbage, I retch and fight off a wave of the dry heaves, another sure sign that I need to get some dope into my body pronto.

No time of year is a good one to be strung out, but the gurgling and irritable bowels of a New York City summer are an especially nasty time, particularly when withdrawal is closing. Once the dope sickness hits with its full force, I'll be sweating, sneezing and feeling bone chillingly cold in ninety-five degree heat.

I'm waiting here for Gavi, as though sitting in my car on 142nd Street will make him materialize faster than hanging out in his apartment with his wife, Madeleine. At least, they have a bedroom with air conditioning.

Five minutes pass. No Gavi.

I drum my fingers on the steering wheel, sniffle and blow my nose.

Ten more minutes elapse. Still, no Gavi.

I toss a Sisters of Mercy CD I stole from the Tower Records where I work into my portable player and turn up the volume. *Black Planet* comes on in sharp and dark counterpoint to the Latino music blaring from open apartment windows and passing cars.

Another fifteen minutes bite the dust. Gavi does not appear.

I punch the steering wheel, turn off *Marianne (Version)*, stash the CD player in the glove box, roll up the windows and get out of the car. A few months ago, when I started coming here after running into Gavi and Madeleine near 125th and Lexington Ave and enlisting them to help me cop dope, I worried that I'd come downstairs and find my car up on blocks.

Now, I'm around here so much that the neighborhood kids keep an eye on the car. The Yemeni guy who runs the bodega on the corner gives me Marlboros, Ring Dings, Twinkies, Ho Hos, Oreos and Diet Coke—nicotine, sugar and caffeine being a junkie's three major food groups—on credit on nights when I'm temporarily out of cash until I steal more CDs from work and sell them the following day.

I climb the stairs in Gavi's building—which smell of piss and Spanish food—and knock on his door again.

Madeleine answers.

"Gavi still no here," she says in her heavily Spanish-accented English.

"I know," I say. "I'm sitting outside in the car."

"I *dunno*' where he is. I hope *nuthin*' happen. I *tol*' you he *lef*' *roun*' one. He was *gonna* go to the meth clinic and to the welfare."

I go into the stiflingly hot living room with Madeleine and sit on the dirty old couch.

Their Pekingese, Nani, is running in circles and barking.

"One o'clock late for the meth clinic and the welfare," she says. "I tol' him go more earlier."

"I can't wait much longer. I'm starting to feel sick."

"*Chu wan' summtin'* to drink? Some food, maybe?"

"No thanks. I might throw up."

"*Wha'* the *las' time chu* gets high?"

"Before I went to work. Around eight this morning."

"*Chu* gets sick *fas'*, Papi."

"I know."

The longest I can go between shots of dope is nine or ten hours, after which, I'm a mess until I get drugs into my system.

"Maybe *chu* should cut down," Madeleine says.

"How am I supposed to do that?"

"How much chu *spen'* a week? Four or *fi' hunred* dollar, no?"

"Yeah."

The problem is that I work in a record store for minimum wage and barely clear $200 a week. This, in turn, means I have to raise two or three hundred dollars a week through non-traditional means like stuffing CDs down my pants and selling them for cash at a used CD store at lunchtime. I average an extra $100 a day this way.

Stealing to get your dope money is far more stressful than writing for a living. I've already almost gotten caught twice leaving the store unusually weighted down.

"You *gotta* work *har'* make that *kinda* money," Madeleine says.

"Tell me about it."

"What *chu gettin* for a CD?"

"Five or six bucks."

"*Thas' alotta'* CD every day, Papi."

A shiver runs through my entire body.

"Yeah," I say, shifting uncomfortably on the couch. "Jesus, Maddi, where is he?"

"Gavi be here. *Dun'* worry. He know what time *chu* alway come. He gonna be back."

"You want to go with me?"

"Gavi know *wha's* out there today."

The Harlem dope market shifts a little every day as new brands hit the street and spots where people sell move around. Gavi's market research helps us cop with as little hassle as humanly possible, which can still be a huge hassle on the wrong day.

"C'mon, Maddi, I'll buy you an extra bag," I say.

Madeleine comes over and sits next to me on the couch, putting her hand on my leg. She's made tentative moves on me several times recently. I'm not in the mood right now and I'm certainly not in the mood for Madeleine, who is married to Gavi, looks at least ten years older than she actually is and is missing several front teeth.

I shift to put distance between us, even though her hand is still on my leg.

"*Chu* gonna tell Gavi *'bou* the extra bag?" Madeleine says.

"No."

"He *fine* out I *goin behine* his back and *gettin* extra dope, he *gonna* be *piss*."

"Don't worry."

"*Chu* gonna get him a bag *anyways*?"

"Sure."

"Maybe we drive *donton* in Manhattan later? We *dun* go *donton* for a long time."

"No problem."

"Nani can come?"

Jesus. This is the junkie version of negotiating a corporate merger.

"Sure," I say. "We always take Nani."

Hearing her name, the dog runs to the door and starts barking.

Madeleine takes her hand from my leg and says, "Okay. *Gimme* a minute to get ready."

Madeleine has been wearing white shorts and a loose orange shirt. She comes back out of the bedroom wearing skin-tight navy blue hot pants and a form fitting white shirt that leave little to the imagination and make her look like she's going out to turn ten-dollar tricks.

We go downstairs with Nani, the Pekinese, running ahead of us. Gavi is still nowhere to be seen as we walk to my car.

I'm sweating, shivering and sneezing as we drive to East 118th Street and First Avenue, near one of the spots where we cop.

I give her money to buy eight bags. Six for me. One for her and one for Gavi.

Shelling out for the extra bag sucks, but it beats getting busted or ripped off.

Madeleine hops out of the car. I pull into a space on First Avenue and wait and wait and wait and wait and wait as I continue to sweat and shiver.

I feel wretched by the time Madeleine comes back thirty minutes later, but I perk up considerably when she hands me eight bags of Fuji Power, a widely available "brand" of dope. A drawing of a soccer ball is stamped on the folded-and-taped bag.

I hand her two bags and put six in my pocket.

I feel instantly better just thinking about shooting up in their bathroom.

I step on it so we can fly up the Harlem River Drive back to 142nd Street and beat back the dog days of August.

Degreasing the New Year

The New Year starts off like the old one—blurry, driven and desperate.

It doesn't skip a beat. All of life erodes into a featureless terrain of hustling up money, hunting down drugs and getting off when you're deep into dope. I was in deep in the Old Year. And, I'm in super deep in the New.

I'm standing on a rooftop in East Harlem with Gavi, looking at a New York City winter vista of Yankee Stadium across the Harlem River in the South Bronx. It's a picture postcard of cold and depressing urban shit.

Gavi's Pekingese, Nani, is a few feet away, squatting to take a crap on the roof.

Gavi passes me a bottle full of *coquito*, a Puerto Rican rum-based holiday concoction he brewed up on New Year's Eve using three bottles of rum I brought him and his wife Madeleine as a present for their East Harlem dope fiend hospitality.

I hang out in their apartment so much that people in the neighborhood no longer give me strange *Who's the White Boy*? looks when I drive up in my old sky blue BMW. The kids on the block keep an eye on the car. The Yemeni guy who runs the bodega on the corner of East 143rd and Lenox Avenue fronts me packs of Marlboros on credit. And the neighbors think I've *moved* into the building, which is midway between a slum dwelling and being abandoned.

Half the apartments are seriously slummy. And half are very abandoned.

The hallways smell like crack, piss and Spanish cooking—*Eau d'East Harlem*. Half of the time, the only heat comes from the kitchen stove because the ancient boiler in the basement only works occasionally. The trash goes out the window into the alley below. The roaches are exemplary New York City ghetto bugs—astounding in size, bold in attitude and awesome in number. And the neighborhood rats are as fearless and brazen as they are monstrously big.

I look at Nani the Pekingese. Having completed taking a dump, the dog is dancing in proud little circles. It is displaying the gratitude a junkie feels after a successful clearing of the bowels because opiates induce constipation that is Biblical in nature.

"Nani," Gavi says in his New Yorican accent.

The dog runs over. Gavi pulls some toilet paper from his pocket, bends over and carefully wipes the dog's ass.

"Good girl," he says.

I consider the bottle of *coquito.* It's cooked up with rum, coconut milk, egg yolks, sugar and vanilla extract. The way Gavi makes it, the *coquito* packs the punch of a freight train.

"Day like this is when the *chit* good," Gavi says. "*Chit* need a day to marinate so all the flavor come out."

I take a hit and nod.

Good chit, indeed.

The *coquito* has definitely matured and filled out in the last forty-eight hours.

I give the bottle back to Gavi. I'm on a lunch break from my telemarketing job, having just sped across the George Washington Bridge and down the Harlem River Drive from Jersey. The plan is to cop and do some dope before I go back to work.

Dope takes the edge off my job. I'm spending my nine-to-fives calling gas stations, machine shops and garages all over the United States trying to sell them huge drums of degreaser.

All I know about degreaser is it degreases things and that I could use a serious degreasing myself right about now, metaphysically if not literally.

They call the basement room where I work in Fort Lee north of the George Washington Bridge, "the boiler room." It contains a dozen tables with two phones each and is presided over by a 5'10", 395-pound Jewish guy from Long Island with four chins named Lou. They call him Jabba the Hutt behind his back. Jabba's second in command is a slight guy with gray hair and a gray beard named Jack. Jack sounds a little like Elmer Fudd and claims to have been a classical musician before he started pimping industrial cleaners for Lou.

No doubt, it's a long and winding road from Carnegie Hall to a basement office in Fort Lee, New Jersey.

My co-workers are a bunch of dope users and drunks (current and former), with one recovering dope fiend and still active degenerate gambler—the guy that hooked me up with the job—thrown in for good measure.

I am, apparently, a big disappointment to the bosses, who shake their heads and tell me every payday that they're going to let me go unless I start moving more degreaser. Jack and Lou keep a chalkboard on the boiler room wall upon which they tally everyone's daily and weekly sales figures. Every time they fire the person whose results are worse than mine, I end up dead last on the board, until an even bigger degreaser slacker comes along.

I am not a good salesman, especially of degreasers.

"May I speak to Earl."

"This is Earl."

"Hi, Earl, my name's Bob. I'm calling from United Chemical Corporation about your order of degreaser!"

"What degreaser?"

Elmer Fudd (Pointing at me and whispering): "Stick to the script."

"The 300-gallon drum you ordered, Earl. It's back in stock and I'm shipping it as soon as you give me the authorization number."

"I didn't order no degreaser."

Elmer Fudd (Gesturing wildly at me): "Of course, he did. Tell him!"

"Of course you did, Earl, but that's not important. I'm giving you an incredible deal on our citrus degreaser."

"You talkin' about that orange shit?"

"Yes, sir. Great! You remember! It's the all-purpose, heavy-duty, citrus degreaser."

"That shit don't clean nuthin'. I ordered a thousand dollars ah the shit last year an' almost lost mah job."

"Oh. I'm so sorry. Wow."

"Don't call no more."

Click.

Elmer Fudd (Shaking his head): "No!!! That's not how you do it! Never let them hang up."

"I'm sorry, Jack. I was on point until the guy said he almost lost his job."

At which point, I head for the john and shoot another bag of dope.

You would too.

I'm a writer—I've even won awards for my journalistic work—but I haven't written a single publishable word in nearly a year. I worked for a big record chain for a while—using the logic that I might as well be near music because I really dig it and I once worked in radio—until the store manager finally caught on that I was taking *beaucoup* CDs, which I would sell at a used CD place on my lunch hour.

Hence, the degreaser gig, which involves neither a cash register to pillage nor merchandise to pilfer. It has resulted in a somewhat more honest lifestyle, except on the occasions when I shoplift because the minimum wage and a dope habit are natural enemies.

I should be grateful for the job, because I'm not exactly a model employee, but I'm not.

I'm bitter and know it will only be a matter of time before I'm busted leaving a CD store with my pants stuffed full of CDs.

Gavi takes another swallow of *coquito* and passes the bottle back to me, but I decline.

"*Wha's* a matter?" he says. "You *dun'* like it?"

"I like it," I say. "But I've got to get back to work after we score."

"You still *wanna'* go score?"

"Yeah. I'll be sick if I wait until later."

"You *mus'* be *gettin'* some *kinda'* long lunch. You *dun'* care about *gettin'* fire?"

"It's just a job."

"*Whatchu gonna'* do, you get fire?"

"Get another job. Hustle some more."

"You *chould* write again, a guy like you."

"I can't," I say. "Not right now. I need a break. I'm burned out."

"You *chould* do less dope, brother."

Jesus Christ. Why do people lecture me about how much dope I do?

Gavi did eight years in Attica prison on a dope charge. He goes to a methadone clinic every morning at nine o'clock. His wife's a methadone addict and on welfare. And I should do less dope?

"I like dope," I say. "It makes me happy."

"Make me happy too," Gavi says. "*Butchu gotta'* watch it, if it fucks *thins* up for you."

"It's not fucking anything up."

"You use *ta* make *lotta'* money, right?"

"Yeah, I guess."

"You *ain't makin' chit* now, right?"

"I'm getting by."

"You *chopliftin'* for money, brother."

"So?" I say.

"You *chus gotta'* think about it is all I'm *sayin'*, you know?"

"Thanks. I appreciate it."

"I'm serious, man. You a nice guy. You *gotta'* good head. You *chould* use it."

"We can talk later. Why don't we go score? I'll be back after work."

We go back downstairs. Gavi puts Nani in the apartment. The dog is whining when we leave. It associates me with going for rides in my car.

We drive down to 123rd and First Avenue. Gavi hops out. I double-park a half block away. He comes back two minutes later and hands me two dimes of Fuji Power dope.

"I'm *gonna'* stay down here," Gavi says. "I still *gotta'* sell my bottles."

Like everybody else, Gavi sells the methadone he gets at the clinic to get money to buy real drugs.

"All right, my friend," I say. "I'll see you later."

I head for a deserted East Harlem street so I can shoot up before another afternoon of pushing degreaser.

White Out

One of the biggest blizzards of my lifetime, by New York City standards, has begun.

A few inches of snow is already on the ground, and the white stuff is coming down so hard you can only see a couple of hundred feet. The over-excited weather people on TV say we're going to get a couple of feet.

Limited visibility.

White out conditions.

A genuine blizzard.

What an awful thing.

Blizzard = Difficulty Procuring Dope.

Difficulty Procuring Dope = Much Prayer on Bended Knees to the Porcelain God.

Blizzard + Difficulty Procuring Dope + Dope Sickness = Complete Human Misery.

Jesus H. Christ.

I should not have set foot out the door. My old BMW fishtails insanely, and I don't know how to drive in snow.

But I could care less about becoming one with a telephone pole or sliding sideways down the highway. I am in my car on Interstate 80, driving like a madman through the building blizzard toward the George Washington Bridge.

Mush.

The car is slippy-sliding, the wipers are freezing and ice is building up on the windshield. A small clear spot, maybe a foot across, is all that I can still see through.

Mush, you BMW Bastard.

I did my last shot of dope an hour ago. Who needs to see, especially when all you can see is snow?

I've got to get over the bridge.

Mush, you German Motherfucker. Mush.

Going Over the Bridge and down the Harlem River Drive will get me to East Harlem where I can get my hands on dope to ride out the storm, even if I've got to ride it out in a cardboard lean-to under the highway.

Without dope, by tonight my stomach will feel like I drank water from a street puddle in Cairo.

Going *mano a mano* with an ass-biting snowstorm is *entirely normal behavior*.

Stocking up on supplies is the traditional response to bad winter weather. For 48 hours, the TV news has featured people filling shopping carts with products:

Milk.

Bread.

Cans of soup.

Bags of rock salt and snow melt.

Etc.

The only difference between them and me is that I don't care about food or snow melt.

If I am to be stranded inside the house for days because of snow up to my ass, my only priority is ensuring that the demanding monkey on my back is fed on the rigid schedule it imposes.

This means using the fifty dollars I have to my name to buy dope before it's too late. Which it may already be.

The average dope dealer is not the kind of guy to hang out on a street corner all day turning into a human snowman in a blizzard so he can move the product and keep the junkies happy. Once the storm is bad enough, most of the cop spots will be quiet and deserted.

The Harlem River Drive is like a bobsled run, but I make it to Gavi's apartment on East 143rd Street without mishap. I have no idea how I will get out of there; most of the exit routes involve going up or down hills so steep they would shock people who picture Manhattan as a flat place.

Getting out is a problem for later.

Right now, I need to retrieve Gavi and get moving.

I go into the filthy lobby and up the dark, cold, piss-and-crack-smelling stairs.

I knock on his door.

Nothing.

Knock. Knock. Knock. Knock.

Again, nothing.

Where could he be in the middle of a snowstorm?

Knock. Knock. Knock. Knock. Knock.

The door opens a crack. When Gavi sees that it's me, he opens the door.

"*Whattchu doin'* here?" he says. "*Snowin'* like crazy. I *wuz* in bed."

"I want to get some dope," I say, walking inside.

I sit on the filthy old sofa. It is against a window that's so drafty it might as well be outside.

"Man," Gavi says. "Snow like this? I *dun* think so."

"What do you mean?"

"I *dun* know who *gonna'* be out. *Prahly* nobody."

"We can try, right?"

"*Chure*, we can try. But it *prahly* too late. You *chould* come more early."

"I was asleep early."

"You don't watch weather?"

"I thought it was going to start later."

"You *chould* watch Eyewitness News. *Ahhkooweather.* Good *chit.* You *gonna'* hit me off with a bag, right?"

Gavi expects payment in kind for his services, but I wasn't planning on it today. I have fifty dollars and God knows how long I'll be snowed in.

"Gavi, I've only got fifty bucks."

"*Whattchu sayin'?*"

"I'm saying I need the money to get five bags for myself. I might be stuck."

"You *chould* plan better. I gonna' be stuck and get sick too."

Gavi's wife, Madeleine, has been standing in the kitchen listening.

"Help him out, Gavi," she says. "*Chu* know Bob good to us."

Damn right I am. I always look out for them.

"Madie," Gavi says. "*Chu* knows we *dun* got no dope."

"We okay," she says. "We drink our meth and we *dun* get too sick."

"Fuck," Gavi says.

"Please?" I say.

"Yeah, okay," Gavi says. "But only *cuz* you a good guy."

"Thanks."

"And I *dun wanttchu doin'* this *chit* no more."

"I'll make it up to you."

All this time, Nani, Gavi's Pekingese has been running around in circles and barking. The dog doesn't know what a dope run is, but she knows that when I show up she goes for a car ride. Nani digs riding in cars.

"Nani can come?" Gavi says.

"Sure," I say. "Nani always comes."

Gavi puts on his coat. The Pekingese charges down the stairs ahead of us.

My car, which is parked out front, has accumulated snow in the brief time I've been inside.

"Where should we go?" I ask Gavi.

"We try 123rd Street *firs'*," he says.

"Good. No hills."

We drive to 123rd Street and First Avenue. Gavi gets out. I drive around the block. When I come back around, Gavi is standing on the corner. I give him a thumbs up, but he shakes his head and motions to me to drive around the block again.

I drive around once. Twice. Three times. Four times.

On circle number ten, Gavi opens the door and gets in the car. He is covered in snow.

"No luck," he says. "Ain't nobody."

"Shit."

"You wanna' try someplace else?"

"Yeah. Where?"

"First we try Lexington."

I drive down Lexington Avenue.

Gavi gets out at several corners, only to return empty-handed.

"Okay," Gavi says. "We try Amsterdam."

Great. The dope spot on Amsterdam Avenue, at West 135th Street, is at the top of huge hill. The only way there is uphill. The only way back is downhill.

Here we go.

Getting to 135th and Amsterdam is like driving up a ski slope. Gavi gets out on a couple of hills and pushes to help get the car moving.

When we get to the block, it is eerily quiet. Gavi tells me to circle the block. Under normal circumstances this would be okay. Today, it involves going down a big hill and coming back up another one.

Gavi get outs. I drive off. The car slides sideways at the bottom of the hill, but I regain control before careening into an oncoming cab. By the time I come around to Amsterdam again, Gavi is standing on the corner. He waves me over and gets in the car.

"*Chu* lucky," he says. "I got five bags. Was a guy in the *buildin'* across the *stree'*. I *hadda'* go inside."

"Great," I say. "Thanks."

I feel better driving back to 143rd and Lennox. I drop Gavi off, figuring that as insane it is to have driven into the city in the first place, it is even crazier to delay driving back to Jersey.

Five bags of dope is enough to get straight for a couple of days, assuming I make it home in one piece.

Six inches of snow is already on the ground and the snow is blowing so hard that it is nearly a white out.

It is definitely time to go.

Drinking (Again)

My brain feels like a twisted iPod that only plays beer commercial MP3s—Heineken, Amstel, Budweiser, Etc.

Unfathomably, the old Rheingold beer jingle is running through my head:

My beer is Rheingold, the dry beer
Think of Rheingold whenever you buy beer
It's refreshing, not sweet
It's the extra dry treat
Won't you try extra dry Rheingold beer?

They stopped brewing Rheingold in Brooklyn in 1976 and I never drank the stuff—despicable piss water favored by the cirrhotic—in my life.

But, I'd kill for one right now.

I haven't had a drink or a drug, as they say, in six months. The drug cravings are under control. The drinking thing, however, is touch and go. I don't break out in a cold sweat every time I walk past a liquor store, bar or club; then again, the urge to have a little drinky-poo pulses through my body about once every 45 seconds after six PM.

Right now, I'm sitting in a café on Avenue A in the East Village drinking another espresso. Two Italian chicks, both about eighteen, are sitting at a table to my right, having an animated discussion.

The Italian chick with black hair in a ponytail and several earrings in each ear is saying something about the *boomps* on her back to the one with a nose ring and flowing brown hair.

The one with the ponytail says she thinks the *soontan* lotion she's using in the *park-a* in *Brooka-lyn* is causing the *boomps* on her *back-a.* She's afraid the *boomps* make her back look *ooghly.* She *looves* her *soontan* but she hates the *boomps.* She is very upset about the *boomps.*

The other Italian chick agrees that *boomps*, especially ones on your back, really suck.

A chick in her early twenties with citrus fruit orange hair is sitting at another table within overhearing distance. Currently, she's waiting for a guy in his late forties with thinning gray hair to return.

"If I peed in a cup, would you drink it?" she asked him a few minutes ago.

He replied that he'd gladly drink her pee. He posted on Craigslist looking for a chick to piss on him, didn't he?

"Well, your ad said 'piss on,' not piss in your mouth or drink my piss," she said.

"I'll really dig your piss any way you give it to me," he said.

The guy split when the girl handed him some cash. Maybe he's gone to cop drugs. Possibly, he went to get a plastic cup like the ones that come with piss tests for drugs. Who knows?

It's like something out of a Jim Jarmusch film. But real and totally and painfully straight.

Ann, who works in the same bookstore as me, is sitting to my left. I've been flirting shamelessly with her for weeks. Her section is Religion and Metaphysics. Mine is Bargain Books. I aspire to Travel because it would allow me to play to my strengths. Fiction would be cool too, but it's too much work. Too many damned people write fiction. A lot less write travel books, even though people that shop for travel books tend to trash the travel section way worse than people looking for fiction.

I'm working in a bookstore because the cognitive dissonance involved with not drinking and/or not doing drugs is making writing impossible, but I still want to be close to the printed word.

In retrospect, this is not a good decision. Bookstores are to writing what paper routes are to reporting. They're not about literature. They're about heavy lifting.

I now know things about bookstores—the ass end of the publishing business—a writer should never have to know.

Ann and I have just Lincoln Tunneled into New York, had Thai food on First Avenue, walked over to Avenue A and sat down in this café across from Tompkins Square Park.

The café's my idea. Ann wants to go to a bar. I'm stalling. I haven't told her I don't drink or do drugs anymore. I should. But I can't. I think it will make me sound like a loser, or even worse, like a reprehensible AA/NA Nazi who could come unglued at any moment.

So, instead of leveling with her, I engage her in a detailed discussion about her favorite drinks. This makes for a long conversation because it is a lengthy list skewed to libations involving vodka and tequila.

White Russians

Stoly on the rocks.

Long Island Ice Teas.

Etc.

And, here we sit.

"Are you ready to go?" she says.

"Huh?" I say.

"Why don't we go to a bar?"

"Let's hang for a few more minutes."

She looks at her cup of coffee, which is nearly empty, and at mine, which is still quite full, and says, "I guess."

Her tone of voice indicates that continuing down this path much longer will be a significant setback in terms of this date.

Getting it over with and having a drink is looking better by the second. Not drinking is for the birds, anyway. My deal is *drugs*. I can't do *drugs* anymore. Drugs like heroin and cocaine. Drugs get me in trouble and take me places I don't want to be. Except for weed, which just makes me sleepy and hungry.

Drinking has never caused me any problems. Except throwing up, passing out and occasionally acting like a moron. But, everybody drinks too much and boots up. It's part of life. Big deal. Eight out of ten people walking down the street at this very moment have probably had a drink in the last several hours.

The anti-drinking thing is NA Twelve Step toad puke propaganda.

Total abstinence. Alcohol is a drug.

Instantly, I make a decision. My New Twelfth Step is *Having gotten a headache and an attitude because of these steps, we came to the conclusion that it was time to go out and have a few for a change.*

Those killjoys need to remember how to party.

"We'll go someplace in a few minutes," I say. "What places do you like?"

Discovery—like learning where someone enjoys drinking—is one of the neat things about hanging out with new people.

Ann names her favorite watering holes south of Fourteenth Street as well as some spots in Williamsburg.

Momentarily, I wonder whether I should really level with her. Tell her the truth. Explain that I'm in an experimental liquor—and drug-free phase for spiritual reasons. Everybody digs and respects spirituality, right?

What if the asswipes from NA are right? Come morning, am I going to be sitting in a puddle of my own puke in a doorway in Harlem nodding out and scratching myself all over?

"Why don't we go to the Mars Bar?" Ann says. The Mars Bar is on Second Avenue, right above East Houston. It's a good place to get so drunk that you won't remember where you've been when you wake up in the morning.

"The Mars Bar?" I say. "Isn't that kind of ten years ago?"

"That's why it's cool."

I am starting to drool, but still trying to put up a fight.

"Let's get more coffee," I say.

"Come on," Ann says.

The Piss Drinker at the other table returns. He sits down next to the chick whose urine he'd like to consume. They kiss. He puts something in the girl's hand. She puts it in her mouth and washes it down with water.

Fuck. It's all around me.

"Let's go someplace where something is *happening*," Ann says.

This is New York. The city so nice, they named it twice. *Something* is always happening *somewhere.*

I am coming to the fork in the road. I will have to take it.

The fact is that I can't turn around without staring at a beer ad. Or go into a restaurant without being asked what I want to drink. Or turn on the radio without hearing the successor to *My beer is Rheingold, the dry beer.*

A fact is a fact is a fact.

And it is time to face facts.

I am *f-u-c-k-e-d.*

"Where you want to go?" I say.

"Doesn't matter," she says. "I'm dying for a drink."

"Yeah, sure. Why not?"

"Good."

I feel energized by my choice.

We leave the café and turn south down Avenue A. It's a glorious summer night, a great night for a drink. Dry air. A cool breeze. A lot of people are out.

We walk past a place with a lot of chrome and big open windows on the street.

"Let's stop here," Ann says.

Well, it's as good a place as any.

"Sure," I say.

We get a table by one of the open windows on Avenue A.

A waitress with an arm covered in tattoos, wearing fishnets and combat boots, comes up and asks what we want to drink.

"Long Island Ice Tea," Ann says.

"Hmm," I say. "Let me think."

The left side of my brain is still saying things like club soda, orange juice and mineral water. I wish it would stop. The right side is saying Stoly on ice. Heineken and a shot of Cuervo. *Fuck that.* Two Heinekens and two shots of Cuervo.

"I don't know," I say.

The waitress is toying with her peroxide blonde hair.

"Club soda," I say.

The waitress starts to walk away.

"Wait a minute," I shout.

The waitress turns around.

"Stoly," I say.

"Stoly or club soda?" she says.

"Stoly and club soda."

She nods.

"No, wait," I say.

Ann gives me a queer look.

The waitress looks peeved.

"Make it a double Stoly. No ice."

Done deal.

The waitress brings the drinks.

I gulp the Stoly like a man who's been walking in the desert. Tastes great. Less filling. I shiver as it goes down.

I look at Ann. She's sipping her drink.

I flag down the waitress and order another round. It is the right thing to do.

ROBERT GUSKIND BIO

Bob Guskind was born on October 19, 1958, and grew up in Clifton, New Jersey. In 1976 Bob was accepted at Georgetown University's College of Arts and Sciences, and graduated in 1980, close to the top of his class (summa cum laude, Phi Beta Kappa).

He immediately was hired by Neal Peirce, one of the founders and then a senior editor of National Journal, in Washington, D.C., and continued writing for the magazine and working with Peirce on his syndicated columns for the Washington Post Writers Group over several years. During these years, Bob also worked with Peirce on many articles on the nation's neighborhood movement and developed the appreciation for neighborhoods that influenced much of his later work. With Peirce, and on commission from the Bruner Foundation, Bob coauthored *Breakthroughs: Re-creating the American City (Rutgers, 1993)*. The book tracked a range of urban success stories ranging from resuscitation campaigns in ravaged New York City and Lincoln, Neb., neighborhoods to the major transit reconstruction of Boston's Southwest Corridor. He also wrote occasional articles for the Washington Post.

After struggling and finally succumbing for several peripatetic years in the 1990s to addiction, Bob reemerged at the new millennium, and worked as the writer, photographer and editor for the weekly newsletter of the New Community Corporation in Newark, NJ. This job was the before-last piece in the puzzle that would eventually coalesce into his infamous blog, *The Gowanus Lounge,* founded in April 2006.

Robert Guskind died March 4th, 2009 of an apparent suicide.

www.ingramcontent.com/pod-product-compliance
Lightning Source LLC
Chambersburg PA
CBHW032003040426
42448CB00006B/472
* 9 7 8 0 9 8 3 0 4 5 6 5 6 *